English

for
Common Entrance

ISEB
Independent Schools
Examinations Board

13+

Practice Book

KORNEL KOSSUTH

HODDER
EDUCATION

www.hoddereducation.co.uk

The publisher would like to thank the following for permission to reproduce copyright material:

Acknowledgments:

Bill Bryson: 'Vienna', abridged from *Neither Here Nor There: Travels in Europe* (Black Swan, 1998), copyright © Bill Bryson 1991; **Charles Causley:** 'Eden Rock' from *Collected Poems* (Macmillan, 1992), copyright © Charles Causley, reproduced by permission of David Higham; **Carol Ann Duffy:** 'Stealing' from *Selling Manhattan* (1987), from *Selected Poems* (Penguin Books, 1994), copyright © Carol Ann Duffy, 1987, 1994; © **Robert Graves:** 'A Boy in Church' from *The Complete Poems in One Volume,* edited by Beryl Graves and Dunstan Ward (Carcanet Press, 2000), reproduced by permission of Carcanet Press; **James Herriot:** 'Bringing the Cows In', abridged from *All Creatures Great and Small* (Pan Books, 1976), copyright © James Herriott 1970, 1972, 1973, reproduced by permission of David Higham; **Phoebe Hesketh:** 'Death of a Gardener' from *The Leave Train: New and Selected Poems* (Enitharmon Press, 1994), © Phoebe Hesketh 1994, reproduced by permission of the publisher; **Khaled Hosseini:** 'Too Soft', abridged from *The Kite Runner* (Bloomsbury Publishing, 2004), copyright © 2003 by Khaled Hosseini; **Ted Hughes:** 'The Thought-Fox' from *New Selected Poems 1957-1994* (Faber & Faber, 1995), © Ted Hughes 1995; **Christopher Logue:** 'War Music' from *War Music. An Account of Books 1-4 and 16-19 of Homer's Iliad* (Jonathan Cape, 1981; Faber & Faber, 2001), © Christopher Logue, 2001; **Cormac McCarthy:** 'Barn Dance' from *All the Pretty Horses* (Picador, 1993), copyright © Cormac McCarthy 1992; **Frank McCourt:** 'The Power of Words', abridged from *Angela's Ashes: A Memoir of a Childhood* (Flamingo, 1997), copyright © Frank McCourt 1996; **Arthur Miller:** 'The Salem Witch Trials Begin', abridged from *The Crucible* (Penguin Classics, 2000), copyright 1952, 1953 by Arthur Miller; **Adrian Mitchell:** 'Especially When It Snows' from *Blue Coffee* (Bloodaxe Books, 1996), © Adrian Mitchell 1996, reproduced by permission of United Agents on behalf of the Estate of Adrian Mitchell; **Evangeline Paterson:** 'The True History of Resurrection Jack' from *The Ring of Words: An anthology of poetry for children,* edited by Roger McGough (Faber & Faber, 1998); **Robert M. Pirsig:** 'Shadow of the Past' from *Zen and the Art of Motorcycle Maintenance. An Inquiry into Values* (Vintage, 1991), copyright © Robert M. Pirsig 1974, 1999; **Sylvia Plath:** 'Goatsucker' from *Collected Poems* (Faber & Faber, 1981), © the Estate of Sylvia Plath; **Vernon Scannell:** 'Legs', abridged from *Collected Poems 1950-1993* (Robson Books, 1993), reproduced by permission of Martin Reed on behalf of the Estate of Vernon Scannell; **T.H. White:** 'A Joust', abridged from *The Once and Future King* (HarperCollins, 1996), copyright © T.H. White, 1939, 1940, 1958; **P.G. Wodehouse:** 'Morning Exercises', abridged from *Something Fresh,* from *Life at Blandings* (Penguin Books, 1981), copyright renewed 1943 by Pelham Grenville Wodehouse.

Every effort has been made to trace and contact all copyright holders, and the publisher will be pleased to make any corrections at the earliest opportunity.

Although every effort has been made to ensure that website addresses are correct at time of going to press, Hodder Education cannot be held responsible for the content of any website mentioned. It is sometimes possible to find a relocated web page by typing in the address of the home page for a website in the URL window of your browser.

Orders: please contact Bookpoint Ltd, 130 Milton Park, Abingdon, Oxon OX14 4SB. Telephone: (44) 01235 827720. Fax: (44) 01235 400454. Lines are open 9.00–17.00, Monday to Saturday, with a 24-hour message answering service. Visit our website at www.hoddereducation.co.uk

© Kornel Kossuth 2014
First published in 2014 by
Hodder Education
An Hachette UK Company,
Carmelite House, 50 Victoria Embankment
London EC4Y 0DZ

| Impression number | 5 | 4 | |
| Year | 2018 | 2017 | 2016 |

Illustrations by Datapage India (Pvt.) Ltd.
Typeset in Bembo Std-Regular 12/14 by Datapage India (Pvt.) Ltd.

Printed in Great Britain for Hodder Education, an Hachette UK Company, Carmelite House, 50 Victoria Embankment London EC4Y 0DZ, by Hobbs the Printers Ltd, Totton, Hampshire, S040 3WX

A catalogue record for this title is available from the British Library

ISBN 978 1 47180411 3

Contents

Introduction

Welcome to this Common Entrance English Practice Book. Packed between the covers of this book are many different exercises to help you practise and prepare for your ISEB 13+ English Common Entrance examination.

The first section of the book contains short exercises that target the specific skills you will need in order to do well in CE (Common Entrance). These are aimed at improving both your comprehension answers as well as your free writing. Most of these exercises will be familiar to those who have already worked through the *Study and Revision Guide*, written by me and also published by Hodder.

The next few chapters each take a section of the exam and give you exam-type practice questions. So you will find five full prose and poetry comprehensions with questions at both levels, the literary prose comprehensions covering a range of genres from (auto)biography to travel writing and novels. In the case of the section Bs there will be a variety of questions.

Recently the syllabus for the English CE exam has changed and there are as yet very few past or practice papers. To make up for this lack of actual CE practice papers, the final section consists of five full mock CE papers with questions for both levels, laid out much like in the exam. The texts for the literary prose comprehension cover all possible genres, including drama.

Although this book is primarily for use in conjunction with the *Study and Revision Guide* (and chapter 1 contains cross-references to this), it can be used independently, too. It can also be used together with the Galore Park ISEB Revision Guide.

My aim in writing this book has been to provide plenty of relevant practice with an answer book that is readily understandable. I hope I have achieved this aim, but if I haven't or you have any suggestions, let me know and I hope to be able to incorporate them in a subsequent edition.

Kornel Kossuth

January 2014

1 Preliminary exercises

Introduction

The following exercises are not part of Common Entrance; they will never appear in a Common Entrance paper. However, they are useful little exercises that focus on developing and testing a specific skill that you will need in the exams. The exercises in this section are designed to improve comprehension techniques as well as how you write. You may have encountered some types of these exercises in the *Study and Revision Guide*, but some are new.

Comprehensions

General exercises

Exercise One – Signal words

Pages 9–13 in the *Study and Revision Guide*

The following exercise tests your knowledge of signal words, and whether you know what type of question is being asked. All you have to do is decide whether the question is a **recall**, **technique**, **thought** or **response** question.

1 How does the author make the football match come to life?

2 The author uses sounds and smells to make the market vivid. Using the text, explain the effects the author creates.

3 In your own words name three things the poet doesn't like about children.

4 Would you like to fly a helicopter? In your answer you should refer to the text where appropriate.

5 What do we learn about the mother in this extract?

6 How does the author intend to gain access to the building? Describe her plan in detail.

7 Would you have acted as the children did? Explain your point of view.

8 How does the author make the description of the people in the tavern vivid?

9 What impression do you gain of the headmaster from the passage?

10 Do you think Jan's escape will be successful?

Exercise Two – How to answer

Pages 14–22 in the *Study and Revision Guide*

The following questions test whether you know what a question requires you to do to answer it correctly. You do not have to provide a full answer, but merely decide what type of question it is and, based on that, say what you would have to do to gain the marks available.

1 How many people are in the car? (1)

2 Do you think the man will be able to round up all the sheep? (6)

3 What kind of a person is the chieftain? Refer closely to the text in your answer. (6)

4 How does the author use sights and sounds to bring the desert to life? (6)

5 What do you think the last line of the poem means? (5)

6 In the extract Jason questions the guide's competence. Do you think Muhammed is a good guide? Explain your reasons in detail. (5)

7 What professions do the author's parents have? (2)

8 In what way is the description of the fight between the mongoose and the cobra effective? (4)

9 How does rhyme add to the effect of the poem? (4)

10 Would you do the same as Frank if you found a million pounds? (4)

Exercise Three – Recall practice

Page 14–15 in the *Study and Revision Guide*

The following exercise tests your ability to answer recall questions.

Read the following passage and then answer the questions that follow it.

There are three different types, or castes, of bees: the queen, the worker and the drone. The queen lays all eggs and keeps the colony together by producing scent markers. Although she is often seen as the head, she does not control the other bees as such. All bees together decide what is best for the colony, though it is not clear how such decisions are reached. The workers are the
5 most common bees in any hive. They are all female and, as their name suggests, do all the work: rearing young, cleaning the hive, guarding entrances and flying out to find nectar and pollen. They literally work themselves to death. Drones are males who do nothing except fertilise new queens, whereupon they die.

1 What are the three types of bees called? (3)

2 Describe in your own words how the queen keeps the colony together. (1)

3 Who rules the colony? (2)

4 In your own words name two things a worker bee does. (2)

5 What do workers usually die of? (1)

6 What happens to drones after they have mated with a queen? (1)

Exercise Four – Explaining imagery

Pages 15–16 in the *Study and Revision Guide*

The following exercise tests your ability to explain similes and metaphors.

Explain the effectiveness of the following images.

1 The maths teacher was an old, grey-haired woman, her face like a bulldog.

2 The blackbirds strutted across the lawn like clockwork.

3 Quivering and shaking like a fly freshly trapped in a spider's web …

4 His heart was thumping like a kettle drum in a vacuum of fear.

5 A bird appeared, cruising lazily like a police car on the prowl.

Exercise Five – Sound effects

Pages 17–18 in the *Study and Revision Guide*

The following exercise tests your ability to explain literary techniques to do with sound.

Explain the effectiveness of the following sound effects.

1 The snow crunched under her feet.

2 Before she reached the door, he struck her to the floor.

3   The iron gate ground to a halt.

4   The bells on her toes jingled.

5   The car bounced along the bumpy boulevard.

Exercise Six – Common techniques

Pages 19–20 in the *Study and Revision Guide*

The following exercise tests your ability to spot and explain how certain common literary techniques achieve their effect in context.

In the following examples name the technique used and explain its effect in the context. Some examples may contain more than one technique; if so, you need only explain one.

1   Let's see what we can do to solve this problem.

2   Do you want to be happy?

3   When I went to town with my sister she bought two pairs of trousers, three blouses, a handbag, a pair of flip-flops and five T-shirts.

4   You may think life will always be easy; you may think someone will always be there to help you along; you may think people will always be friendly to you; you may think that the world is just waiting for you.

5   Peter was standing, watching his son slowly walk away, staring at the marbles in his hand. Suddenly Peter feels a tap on his shoulder.

6   Unless you start recycling now, the world will return to the dark ages in the next ten years.

7   What once was said can't fly again,
With time the words I'd use have lost their light:
Another love song I won't write.

8   Don't waste your time; start writing immediately.

9   Ball in hand Hal started running for the try line, the opposition in hot pursuit. He dodged round the legs of the other team like quicksilver, always slipping through their guard. Panting heavily, legs pumping, focusing only on the line, Hal sprinted the last few feet. Suddenly, he slipped.

10 'How could you do THAT to me?' she screamed.

Exercise Seven – Inferring character

Pages 20–22 in the *Study and Revision Guide*

The following exercise tests your ability to answer some types of thought questions by inferring character from situations.

Explain which characteristic each of these sentences demonstrates.

1   Although the Cimbri had slaughtered many Roman soldiers, when the prisoners were brought before him, Caesar did not have them executed, but let them return home under oath never to take up arms against Rome again.

2   When Isabel saw her boyfriend laughing with another girl she walked over to them and pretended to slip, spilling her drink all over the girl.

3   Although Jeff had come to the shop only to buy some milk, when he saw the ice creams by the counter, he immediately bought one.

4   Even though the question of the headmistress was not clear, Caspar told her everything he knew about the incident, even mentioning his slightly dubious role in the matter.

5   Holly was quick to laugh at Alice when the other girls made fun of her, but when Holly failed her maths exam, Alice comforted her.

6   James knew that he was not the favourite to be elected form prefect, so weeks before the vote he started spreading false rumours about the other candidates and getting them caught in situations that made them look bad, but in a way that no-one would suspect him.

7   The pupils shouted in outrage when they were told that they had to re-do the prep, but Eva remained silent, checking through her exercise book, trying to find out where she had gone wrong.

8   While watching the cricket match, David lost focus as he stared at the clouds, trying to detect shapes in them and imagining what would happen if they came alive.

Exercise Eight – Stairway to heaven

Pages 34–35 in the *Study and Revision Guide*

This exercise is designed to extend your vocabulary.

Look at the following words. Each one has more than one meaning (its various meanings are homonyms). For each meaning of each word, write one sentence that shows what the word means. If you are particularly daring or playful, you could try putting all the different meanings of one homonym into one sentence. If you are unsure of all the meanings of a word, use a dictionary.

Example: brood

   (a) The worker bees start their lives looking after the brood, making sure the larvae are fed and kept at a constant temperature.

   (b) When faced with a problem, he is apt to brood and let dark thoughts enter his head rather than get up and do something to resolve the situation.

   (c) The hen brooded on her nest, keeping the egg warm beneath her.

1   fast

2   apt

3   bow

4   pole

5   bear

6   follow

7   bark

8   change

9   order

10 trunk

11 row

Exercises for Poetry Comprehensions

Exercise Nine – Get rhythm

Pages 39–41 in the *Study and Revision Guide*

The following exercise tests your ability to recognise rhythm patterns.

Find the rhythm in the following lines. Note that the rhythm will not necessarily be regular.

1   If ever I lay my hands on the brazen burglar …

2   The rattlesnake hissed mercilessly at the frightened squirrel.

3   The wizard knew his time had come.

4   … fluffy little bunnies running madly …

5   If the wave hits the boat we will drown in the swell.

6 The captain was afraid of crocodiles.

7 Nocturnal creatures often use their hearing to find their prey.

Exercise Ten – Rhyme time

Pages 42–43 in the *Study and Revision Guide*

This exercise tests your knowledge of rhymes and rhyme patterns.

Name the type of rhyme or the rhyme pattern in the following words or lines.

1 hare/stair

2 There was an old fellow from Ealing
Who always stared up at the ceiling;
They called doctors and vicars
And other nit pickers,
But they'd no clue with what they were dealing.

3 part/started

4 knuckle/pickle

5 One day I'd like to go to town
To buy a pair of shoes,
A purple satin dressing gown
And fluffy slippers too.

6 This isn't how it's meant to be:
That should be land and this the sea.

Writing tasks

General exercises

Exercise One – Making sense of sentences

Pages 50–51 in the *Study and Revision Guide*

The following exercise tests your ability to formulate correct sentences that make complete sense.

Look at the following fragments and turn them into sentences that make sense.

1 Humming a tune to himself, walking through the cityscape, watching the people stream by.

2 He had cornered the enemy ready to kill him while he drew his gun knowing that this might be end.

3 He pressed him to the floor losing consciousness.

4 The gloomy light seeping through.

5 Tapping against the window, he looked at the trees swaying madly in the wind thinking why was he here.

6 Running through the heather so bright and purple stretched out to the horizon as far as I could see.

7 Because he was busy, he doesn't see the men thinking that he is safe in the home alarms protecting him.

Exercise Two – Making sure there were no there were

Page 52 in the *Study and Revision Guide*

This exercise is to help you improve your style.

Re-write the following sentences, so that you replace 'there was/were/is/are' with more exciting choices.

1   There was a crowd of people demonstrating in the city.

2   There were many books lying scattered around on the library tables.

3   There were many cows in the field.

4   There was a slight problem.

5   There is no way out of this prison.

Exercise Three – Tightening prose

Pages 52–53 in the *Study and Revision Guide*

This exercise is to help you improve your style and to make sure you do not use any unnecessary words.

Tighten the following passage.

Running scared through the woods as quickly as my legs would carry me, the boughs tugging at my shirt, I knew I had to get out of here if I wanted to make it home. Most of the light had gone and the forest was dark so that I could barely see anything. I could hardly see my hands in front of me. As I ran branches whipped across my bare arms and face, stinging my face and arms. It hurt
5 like wires of heat being wrapped around me, but I kept on running. I was not sure which direction I was going, because it was so dark, but I kept on, thinking if I continue in one direction I must get out. Suddenly I stumbled on a root that had snaked out onto the path as if to trip me up on purpose. I went flying and my ankle twisted beneath me. I was in pain and screamed. Now I knew I would no longer be able to run because of the pain in my ankle.

Prose for a purpose

Exercise Four – Beginnings

Pages 57–59 in the *Study and Revision Guide*

This exercise tests your ability to write introductions to practical prose pieces.

Write all six kinds of introduction (and the introduction only) for the following title:

Pupils have to sit too many exams.

Note: The six types of introduction are:
- own experience
- current affairs or historical link
- definition of the title
- proverb or saying
- cultural link
- repeat title in own words.

Exercise Five – The end

Pages 71–72 in the *Study and Revision Guide*

The following exercise tests your ability to write conclusions based on a plan.

Look carefully at each plan and then write a conclusion for each one. Remember that the conclusion for an informative essay should summarise the main points and then show a way forward (possibly where you can obtain more information), while the conclusion to an essay about books should highlight the underlying issue or throw a different light on the question.

Plan 1

Title: How do you spend your holidays?

Main points   More detail   Fine points

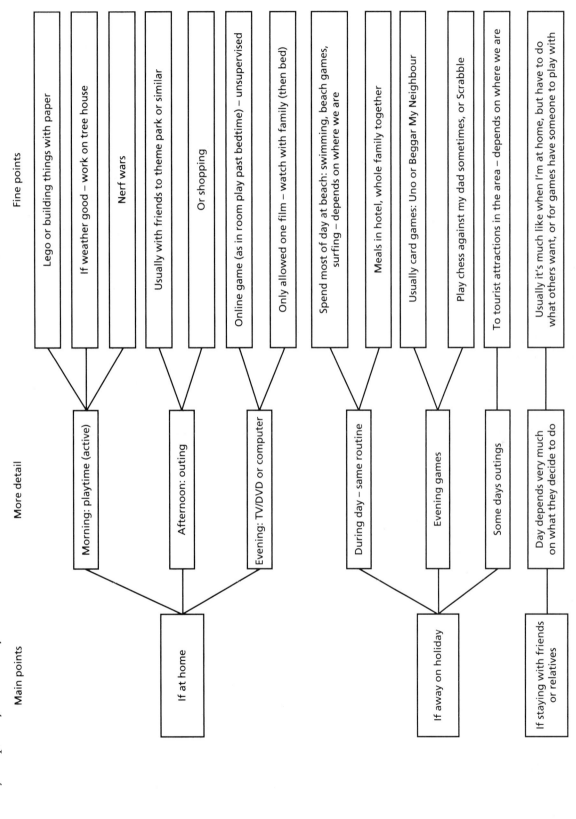

If at home
- Morning: playtime (active)
  - Lego or building things with paper
  - If weather good – work on tree house
  - Nerf wars
- Afternoon: outing
  - Usually with friends to theme park or similar
  - Or shopping
- Evening: TV/DVD or computer
  - Online game (as in room play past bedtime) – unsupervised
  - Only allowed one film – watch with family (then bed)

If away on holiday
- During day – same routine
  - Spend most of day at beach: swimming, beach games, surfing – depends on where we are
  - Meals in hotel, whole family together
- Evening games
  - Usually card games: Uno or Beggar My Neighbour
  - Play chess against my dad sometimes, or Scrabble
- Some days outings
  - To tourist attractions in the area – depends on where we are

If staying with friends or relatives
- Day depends very much on what they decide to do
  - Usually it's much like when I'm at home, but have to do what others want, or for games have someone to play with

Plan 2

Title: A good book will always make you think

	Scene 1	Scene 2	Scene 3
Summary	Midsummer Night's Dream: Mechanicals in wood rehearsing play: Bottom wants to play all parts (roars like lion etc.).	Private Peaceful: Tommo finds out that Molly and Charlie have been writing love letters and meeting in secret.	Holes: Stanley has to dig holes in Camp Green Lake that are always of certain size and depth as punishment.
Answer to title	Shakespeare undoubtedly 'good book' – this scene does not make me think, but just laugh and enjoy myself. It is slapstick almost.	Scene makes me think about loyalty and love: Tommo and Charlie (brothers!) both love Molly and Molly friends with Tommo, but loves Charlie. What should Molly and Charlie have done?	You wonder why he has to do that (suspense), but you also question whether Stanley's punishment is fair. Even if he had stolen the trainers, should he have to dig holes in the heat with poisonous lizards around?
Why scenes similar/ different	Characters aren't faced with a decision or difficult situation. Comedy here is for relief. Scene is well written and way Bottom misuses language is worth looking at. Mechanicals not main characters, so we don't care for them as much.	Scene is about important emotions and characteristics. It's a situation we could all be in (or similar) and thus we relate to it. Because we care about characters, we don't want them to get hurt and wonder how this could have been avoided.	We've all made little mistakes or been wrongly blamed for doing something bad. We thus can relate to Stanley. It also makes us think how lucky we are to not be punished like that and how unfair the system in 'Holes' is. Stanley main character, so we care about him.

Creative writing

Exercise Six – A different spin

Page 78 in the *Study and Revision Guide*

This exercise tests your ability to re-interpret a given title. Look at the following titles and for each one try to find as many different and unusual ways of writing about it as possible.

1 A Day in the Sun

2 Behind the Door

3 My Favourite Teacher

4 The Waiting-Room

5 Break

Exercise Seven – Different beginnings

Page 80 in the *Study and Revision Guide*

This exercise tests your ability to write various exciting openings for stories.

Write all four kinds of beginning (the first two or three sentences only) for the following title:

The Disused Station

Note: The four types of beginning are:
- dialogue
- onomatopoeia
- setting
- mystery

Exercise Eight – Extending similes

Pages 82–83 in the *Study and Revision Guide*

The following exercise tests your ability to write exciting similes.

Look at the similes below, which are all purposefully dull. Make them more exciting by adding more detail.

1 Leaves swirled in the air like bits of paper.

2 In his anger he shouted as loudly as a thunderstorm.

3 The rose was as red as blood.

4 The clouds rushed across the sky like sailing boats.

5 She stood as still as a statue.

6 The thief moved as stealthily as a mouse.

2 Literary prose comprehensions

Introduction

This chapter contains five literary prose comprehensions. It is designed to give you specific practice for Paper 1, Section A of the exam. According to the new exam board syllabus, the passage that these comprehension exercises are based on can be taken from a novel, a play, a biography or travel writing. All of these genres are represented either in these five exercises or in the full mock papers contained in Chapter 7, ensuring as complete a preparation as possible.

The layout of these comprehension exercises closely reflects how they are presented in the exam itself, to make practice as realistic as possible. *However, precedence has been given to Level 2, so these questions face the texts and the Level 1 questions are overleaf.* If you are practising Level 1 it is advisable to photocopy the questions and place them over the Level 2 ones, so you, too, have the questions facing the text.

The questions and marks all mirror current exam board practice.

At the end of each set of questions is a short explanation on how to approach a text and what to look out for while reading it in an exam situation. The aim of this is to help you tune your brain to what you need to be doing and working out while reading an extract.

When working through each exercise bear in mind the following:
- You have about 35 minutes to complete each comprehension exercise, which includes reading and note-making time.
- You should answer all questions.
- Language, spelling, grammar, punctuation and presentation are important.

Shadow of the Past

Robert Pirsig used to be a university professor until he had a breakdown. During his treatment the person he used to be was destroyed to a large degree. In this extract Pirsig and his son Chris return to the university where he used to teach and he wonders about his former self who he refers to in the third person.

Not many people seem to be around. There wouldn't be, of course. Summer session is on now. Huge and strange gables over old dark-brown brick. A beautiful building, really. The only one that really seems to belong here. Old stone stairway up to the doors. Stairs cupped by wear from millions of footsteps.

5   'Why are we going inside?'

'Shh, just don't say anything now.'

I open the great heavy outside door and enter. Inside are more stairs, worn and wooden. They creak underfoot and smell of a hundred years of sweeping and waxing. Halfway up I stop and listen. There's no sound at all.

10   Chris whispers, 'Why are we here?'

I just shake my head. I hear a car go by outside.

Chris whispers, 'I don't like it here. It's scary in here.'

'Go outside then,' I say.

'You come too.'

15   'Later.'

'No, now.' He looks at me and sees I'm staying. His look is so frightened I'm about to change my mind, but then suddenly his expression breaks and he turns and runs down the stairs and out the door before I can follow him.

The big heavy door closes down below, and I'm all alone here now. I listen for some sound ....
20 Of whom? ... Of *him?* ... I listen for a long time …

The floorboards have an eerie creak as I move down the corridor and they are accompanied by an eerie thought that it is him. In this place he is the reality and I am the ghost. On one of the classroom doorknobs I see his hand rest for a moment, then slowly turn the knob, then push the door open.

25   The room inside is waiting, exactly as remembered, as if he were here now. He is here now. He's aware of everything I see. Everything jumps forth and vibrates with recall.

The long dark-green chalkboards on either side are flaked and in need of repair, just as they were. The chalk, never any chalk except little stubs in the trough, is still here. Beyond the blackboard are the windows and through them are the mountains he watched, meditatively, on days when the
30 students were writing. He would sit by the radiator with a stub of chalk in one hand and stare out the window at the mountains, interrupted, occasionally, by a student who asked, 'Do we have to do … ?' And he would turn and answer whatever thing it was and there was a oneness he had never known before. This was a place where he was received – as himself. Not as what he could be or should be but as himself. A place all receptive – listening. He gave everything to it. This wasn't one room, this
35 was a thousand rooms, changing each day with the storms and snows and patterns of clouds on the mountains, with each class, and even with each student. No two hours were ever alike, and it was always a mystery to him what the next one would bring …

Read the passage entitled 'Shadow of the Past' which is taken from Zen and the Art of Motorcycle Maintenance by Robert Pirsig and answer the questions that follow at the appropriate level, using complete sentences.

The marks given for each question are a guide as to how much you should write in your answers.

LEVEL 2 questions

1   Name three things the author mentions as not having changed in the classroom he used to teach in.   (3)

2   How does the author make the university seem uncanny in lines 1–9? You should refer closely to the text in your answer.   (4)

3   How does the author bring across the strangeness of being where he used to be as a person he no longer is?   (6)

4   What do we learn about the character of the author from this extract? You should use short quotations to support your answers.   (6)

5   Explain in as much detail as you can in which way his classroom was not one room, but 'a thousand rooms' (line 35).   (6)

LEVEL 1 questions

1   Look at lines 27–30. What three things does the author mention as not
     having changed in the classroom he used to teach in?   (3)

2   In lines 1–9 the author makes the university seem uncanny.

     (a)   Write down two quotations that show how the author does this.   (2)

     (b)   Explain your choices.   (4)

3   (a)   Write down two quotations from lines 21–26 that show the
           strangeness the author feels at being where he used to teach, but
           as a person he no longer is.   (2)

     (b)   For each of your quotations explain in detail how the author
           creates this sense of strangeness.   (4)

4   What impression do you gain of the author? Find and explain two
     quotations that tell you something about the author's character.   (2+4)

5   What do you think the author means when he says his classroom was
     not one room, but 'a thousand rooms' (line 35)?   (4)

Notes on the text

The information at the beginning of the extract tells you it's about Pirsig and the introduction to the questions tells you the text was written by Pirsig. This means the text is taken from an autobiography.

The narrator of the passage is therefore Robert Pirsig, a real person.

Knowing this, you can expect the setting to be realistic, but some time back. So do not expect internet or mobile phones, computer games or such technology, but do expect real-life concerns.

The introduction to the text tells you that the Pirsig writing the book is in many ways different from the person Pirsig used to be. As the author is re-visiting a place of the past, expect a lot of thoughts about his past life and who he used to be.

In the first five lines Pirsig is describing the building, obviously as he walks up to it. Subsequently he has a discussion with Chris about whether to go in or not.

It is important to gauge the atmosphere correctly here: Chris is obviously uneasy (he says 'It's scary' – line 12) and he doesn't want to go in (and in fact doesn't). The author also finds the atmosphere eerie (the stairs creak, he stops to listen and he is ready to leave when he realises how scared Chris is). But for him there is more at stake: he wants to try to find out something about the person he used to be, so he presses on.

Lines 19–24 are pivotal in that memories and reality mix and he suddenly no longer seems sure about who he is: the person he now is, or the person he used to be. This is all the more understandable as physically he is the same person, though in his mind he isn't. Pirsig brings across the distinction between the person he was and himself now, by referring to his past self as 'he' and his present self as 'I'.

However, even if you do not understand this central part, you can still work with the final paragraph as a description of someone revisiting a classroom they used to teach in. The only thing to bear in mind is that the 'he' being referred to is, in fact, the author himself, as the introduction explains.

Morning Exercises

He was a tall, well-built, fit-looking young man, with a clear eye and a strong chin; and he was dressed, as he closed the front door behind him, in a sweater, flannel trousers, and rubber-soled gymnasium shoes. In one hand he bore a pair of Indian clubs, in the other a skipping-rope.

Having drawn in and expelled the morning air in a measured and solemn fashion, he laid down
5 his clubs, adjusted his rope, and began to skip.

When one considers how keenly London, like all large cities, resents physical exercise, unless taken with some practical and immediate utilitarian object in view, this young man's calm, as he did this peculiar thing, was amazing. The rules governing exercise in London are clearly defined. You may run, if you are running after a hat, or an omnibus; you may jump, if you do so with the idea of
10 avoiding a taxi-cab or because you have stepped on a banana-skin. But, if you run because you wish to develop your lungs or jump because jumping is good for the liver, London punishes you with its mockery. It rallies round and points the finger of scorn.

Yet this morning, Arundell Street bore the spectacle absolutely unmoved. The whole thing affords a remarkable object-lesson of what a young man can achieve with patience and perseverance.

15 The first time he appeared in Arundell Street in his sweater and flannels, he had barely whirled his Indian clubs once round his head before he had attracted the following audience:

(a) two cabmen (one intoxicated);

(b) four waiters from the Hotel Mathis;

(c) six waiters from the Hotel Previtali;

20 (d) six chambermaids from the Hotel Mathis;

(e) five chambermaids from the Hotel Previtali;

(f) the proprietor of the Hotel Mathis;

(g) the proprietor of the Hotel Previtali;

(h) a street-cleaner;

25 (i) eleven nondescript loafers;

(j) twenty-seven children;

(k) a cat.

They all laughed, even the cat, and kept on laughing.

A month later, such is the magic of perseverance, his audience had narrowed down to the
30 twenty-seven children. They still laughed, but without that ringing conviction which the sympathetic support of their elders had lent them.

And now after three months, the neighbourhood, having accepted Ashe and his morning exercises as a natural phenomenon, paid him no further attention.

On this particular morning, Ashe Marson skipped with even more than his usual vigour. This
35 was because he wished to expel by means of physical fatigue a small devil of discontent of whose presence within him he had been aware ever since getting out of bed.

Skipping brought no balm. He threw down his rope, and took up the Indian clubs.

Indian clubs left him still unsatisfied. The thought came to him that it was a long time since he had done his Larsen Exercises. Perhaps they would heal him.

40 Larsen's Exercises are the last word in exercises. They bring into play every sinew of the body. They promote a brisk circulation. They enable you, if you persevere, to fell oxen, if desired, with a single blow.

But they are not dignified. Indeed, to one seeing them suddenly and without warning for the first time, they are markedly humorous. The only reason why King Henry of England, whose son sank with the White Ship, never smiled again, was because Lieutenant Larsen had not then invented his
45 admirable Exercises.

(abridged)

Read the passage entitled 'Morning Exercises' which is taken from Something Fresh *(first published in 1915) by* P. G. Wodehouse and answer the questions that follow at the appropriate level, using complete sentences.

The marks given for each question are a guide as to how much you should write in your answers.

LEVEL 2 questions

1   In your own words summarise the rules governing exercise in London.   (2)

2   Look at lines 17–33. How does the author make the reaction of the Londoners to Ashe's exercises humorous?   (6)

3   How does Ashe make his neighbourhood accept his exercise routine? You should describe the steps in detail.   (4)

4   What kind of a person is Ashe? In your answer you should refer closely to the text.   (6)

5   (a)   Why does Ashe decide to do Larsen Exercises?   (1)

      (b)   Explain in detail what kind of exercises the Larsen Exercises are.   (6)

LEVEL 1 questions

1   Look at lines 7–13.

    (a) For which reasons are you allowed to run or jump in London? (2)

    (b) For which reasons should you not run or jump in London? (2)

2   (a) Write down three quotations from the passage that you find humorous. (3)

    (b) Explain your choices briefly. (3)

3   How does Ashe make his neighbourhood accept his exercise routine? Describe what he does in as much detail as possible. (4)

4   What kind of a person is Ashe? In your answer you should use and explain quotations. (6)

5   What do you learn about the Larsen Exercises from the passage? (5)

Notes on the text

The introduction tells you that the story was first published in 1915. This means, while there would be telephone and cars, only the rich would have been able to afford them. Society was more structured and the upper class had many servants to run their household.

The text is written by P. G. Wodehouse, who is famous for his Jeeves novels. Even if you do not know this, the fact that the passage is about Ashe Marson, and the way it is written, suggest this is fiction.

The extract begins with a simple description. With the beginning of the third paragraph you should realise that the passage is intended to be humorous: the writing is overdone and exaggerated in its precision and willingness to explain, and its content is light-hearted.

From this moment on, you should not take the author too seriously and also be on the lookout for humorous techniques. One thing to also realise is that a hallmark of humour is to spend a lot of time giving irrelevant information as it is funny, but this also builds up the contrast that is necessary for humour to flourish. Thus, lines 7–13 and 42–47 have little or nothing to do with the plot, but add to the humour. Do not mistake them for elements of the story.

The list starting on line 19 is unusual. As such you should realise it is meant to be humorous.

P. G. Wodehouse writes in a style that uses a lot of carefully chosen words for various effects. It does not necessarily always matter if you do not understand each and every one of them, as long as you understand the gist of what he is saying.

A Joust

The young King Arthur, nicknamed the Wart, and his tutor, Merlyn the magician, watch two knights, King Pellinore and Sir Grummore, engage in a friendly joust.

Without further words, the gentlemen retreated to the opposite ends of the clearing, *fewtered their spears, and prepared to hurtle together in the preliminary charge.

'I think we had better climb this tree,' said Merlyn. 'You never know what will happen in a joust like this.'

5   To be able to picture the terrible battle which now took place there is one thing which ought to be known. A knight in his full armour of those days was generally carrying as much as or more than his own weight in metal. He often weighed no less than twenty-two stone, and sometimes as much as twenty-five. This meant that his horse had to be a slow and enormous weight-carrier, like the farm horse of today, and that his own movements were so hampered by his burden of iron and padding
10 that they were toned down into slow motion, as on the cinema.

'They're off!' cried the Wart, holding his breath with excitement.

Slowly and majestically, the ponderous horses lumbered into a walk. The spears, which had been pointing in the air, bowed to a horizontal line and pointed at each other. King Pellinore and Sir Grummore could be seen to be thumping their horses' sides with their heels for all they were worth,
15 and in a few minutes the splendid animals had shambled into an earth-shaking imitation of a trot. Clank, rumble, thump-thump went the horses, and now the two knights were flapping their elbows and legs in unison, showing a good deal of daylight in their seats. There was a change in tempo, and Sir Grummore's horse could be definitely seen to be cantering. In another minute King Pellinore's was doing so too. It was a terrible spectacle.

20   'Now!' cried the Wart.

With a blood-curdling beat of iron hoofs the mighty equestrians came together. Their spears wavered for a moment within a few inches of each other's helms and then they were galloping off in opposite directions. Sir Grummore drove his spear deep into the beech tree where they were sitting, and stopped dead. King Pellinore, who had been run away with, vanished altogether behind his
25 back.

'Is it safe to look?' inquired the Wart, who had shut his eyes at the critical moment.

'Quite safe,' said Merlyn. 'It will take them some time to get back in position.'

'Whoa, whoa, I say!' cried King Pellinore in muffled and distant tones, far away among the gorse bushes.

30   'Hi, Pellinore, hi!' shouted Sir Grummore, 'Come back, my dear fellah. I'm over here.'

There was a long pause, while the complicated stations of the two knights readjusted themselves.

They fewtered their spears again, and thundered into the charge.

'Oh,' said the Wart, 'I hope they don't hurt themselves.'

35   But the two mounts were patiently blundering together, and the two knights had simultaneously decided on the sweeping stroke. Each held his spear at right angles toward the left, and, before the Wart could say anything further, there was a terrific yet melodious thump. Clang! went the armour, like a motor omnibus in collision with a smithy, and the jousters were sitting side by side on the green *sward, while their horses cantered off in opposite directions.

40   'A splendid fall,' said Merlyn.

(abridged)

Glossary

*fewter – to rest the lance so it is pointing at the opponent

*sward – an area of lush grassland

Read the passage entitled 'A Joust' which is taken from The Once and Future King *by T. H. White and answer the questions that follow at the appropriate level, using complete sentences.*

The marks given for each question are a guide as to how much you should write in your answers.

LEVEL 2 questions

1   Describe, in your own words, the 'sweeping stroke' (line 36).   (2)

2   Describe in detail the various phases of the joust.   (4)

3   (a)   How does the author bring the battle between the knights to life?   (6)

   (b)   How do the Wart's comments add tension to the description of
          the joust?   (4)

4   The extract is quite humorous. Write down two quotations that you
     think are comical and explain their effect.   (4)

5   Does the description in the extract differ from what you thought a joust
     would be like? Explain your answer in detail.   (5)

LEVEL 1 questions

1   What is the 'sweeping stroke' (line 36)?   (2)

2   There are four distinct parts to the battle between King Pellinore and
    Sir Grummore (lines 12–40). Describe each phase briefly.   (4)

3   A simile is a comparison using 'like' or 'as'; onomatopoeia is when a
    word sounds like what it is describing.

    (a)   Find an example of each from the battle scene (lines 12–40).   (2)

    (b)   Explain the effect of each in as much detail as possible.   (4)

4   (a)   Write down three quotations from the passage that you find
          humorous.   (3)

    (b)   Explain briefly in what way your chosen quotations are comical.   (3)

5   Does the description in the extract differ from what you thought a joust
    would be like? Explain your answer.   (4)

Notes on the text

The introduction to the text tells you this is a story about King Arthur, so it's definitely fiction. The fact that Arthur is nicknamed 'the Wart' suggests this is an unconventional version of events, as King Arthur is usually seen as majestic and lofty, neither of which the Wart is – quite the contrary.

The extract has a little comment by the author in lines 5–10, which serves to set the scene and explain happenings, so the reader can better picture them.

After this passage, in which the author tells the reader that jousts were not high-speed collisions, but more lumbering affairs, the subsequent descriptions (lines 12–19 and 35–39) are all tinged with gentle irony about the speed of the joust. You should therefore realise that phrases like 'terrible spectacle' (line 19) and 'blood-curdling' (line 21) are not necessarily to be taken at face value.

You should realise that lines 23–25 are meant to be funny, as the tension of the knights charging together is released in them both missing one another and having some mishap. In tone this is slap-stick humour. This tone continues in lines 35–39.

Note how the author writes a paragraph of description, then uses dialogue to make the scene immediate and then describes again.

The Power of Words

Frank McCourt grew up in the slums of Limerick, Ireland, and in this extract is working as a telegram boy.

There's a telegram for an old woman, Mrs. Brigid Finucane. She says, How old are you, by?

Fifteen and a half, Mrs. Finucane.

Are you smart, by? Are you anyway intelligent?

I can read and write, Mrs. Finucane.

5 Can you write a letter?

I can.

She wants me to write letters to her customers. If you need a suit or dress for your child you can go to her. She gives you a ticket to a shop and they give you the clothes. She gets a discount and charges you the full price and interest on top. You pay her back weekly. Some of her customers

10 fall behind in their payments and they need threatening letters. She says, I'll give you threepence for every letter you write and another threepence if it brings a payment. If you want the job come here on Thursday and Friday nights, and bring your own paper and envelopes.

I'm desperate for that job. I want to go to America.

In a large ledger she gives me the names and addresses of six customers behind in their

15 payments. Threaten 'em, by. Frighten the life out of 'em.

My first letter,

Dear Mrs. O'Brien,

Inasmuch as you have not seen fit to pay me what you owe me I may be forced to resort to legal action. There's your son, Michael, parading around the world in his new suit which I paid

20 for while I myself have barely a crust to keep body and soul together. I am sure you don't want to languish in the dungeons of Limerick jail far from friends and family.

I remain, yours in litigious anticipation,
Mrs. Brigid Finucane

She tells me, That's a powerful letter, by, better than anything you'd read in the *Limerick*

25 *Leader*. That word, inasmuch, that's a holy terror of a word. What does it mean?

I think it means this is your last chance.

I write five more letters and she gives me money for stamps. On my way to the post office I think, Why should I squander money on stamps when I have two legs to deliver the letters myself in the dead of night? When you're poor a threatening letter is a threatening letter no matter how it comes in the door.

30 I run through the lanes of Limerick shoving letters under doors, praying no one will see me.

The next week Mrs. Finucane is squealing with joy. Four of 'em paid. Oh, sit down now and write more, by. Put the fear of God in 'em.

Week after week my threatening letters grow sharper and sharper. I begin to throw in words I hardly understand myself.

35   Dear Mrs. O'Brien,

    Inasmuch as you have not succumbed to the imminence of litigation in our previous epistle be advised that we are in consultation with our barrister above in Dublin.

    Next week Mrs. O'Brien pays. She came in tremblin' with tears in her eyes, by, and she promised she'd never miss another payment.

    (abridged)

Read the passage entitled 'The Power of Words', which is taken from Angela's Ashes *by Frank McCourt, and answer the questions that follow at the appropriate level, using complete sentences.*

The marks given for each question are a guide as to how much you should write in your answers.

LEVEL 2 questions

1   Describe in your own words how Mrs Finucane makes money.   (3)

2   How does Frank make the letters threatening?   (6)

3   In what way do you think this extract shows that words have power?
     Use quotations to support your ideas.   (4)

4   What impression do you have of the author from this extract? You
     should refer closely to the text in your answer.   (6)

5   How does the author bring the experiences of his childhood in Limerick
     to life?   (6)

LEVEL 1 questions

1   Explain briefly why people might go to Mrs Finucane for money.   (4)

2   Frank uses a number of persuasive techniques to make his letters
    threatening.

    (a)   Write down two quotations (not those in Question 3, though) that
          you think are effective in persuading people to pay.   (2)

    (b)   Explain your choices in detail.   (4)

3   In what way do you think the following words, used in the extract, are
    powerful? You should write a brief explanation for each phrase.

    Inasmuch (line 18 and 36), litigious anticipation (line 22), imminence
    of litigation (line 36), epistle (line 36), in consultation with our barrister
    (line 37)   (5)

4   What kind of person is the author? Write down two quotations about
    the author from the passage and explain what they tell you about him.   (2+4)

5   The author obviously has a difficult childhood in Limerick. How does
    the author make this clear? You should write down two quotations and
    briefly explain what they tell you.   (4)

Notes on the text

The extract is about Frank McCourt and is written by him (as the introduction to the questions tells you) – this is therefore autobiographical writing. The narrator is Frank McCourt, an actual person.

The introduction tells you that the setting is in a poor area of Ireland, so expect poverty and deprivation on a scale you would not think possible nowadays. The time is not specified, but the fact that Frank is working as someone who delivers telegrams suggests this is definitely before the 1960s.

The first thing you should notice is that the author does not use any speech marks. This makes it more difficult to pick out speech, but new lines should give you a clue. Another clue to discovering what is speech and what not, is the use of colloquialisms in the speech, so for example the dropping of the 'g' at the end of some words.

Lines 7–9 explain Mrs Finucane's business in detail. This is quite complex and you don't have to understand this exactly to work with the extract. What is important is that you realise that poor people owe her money and do not always pay on time, which is why Frank has to write them threatening letters.

In the letters Frank uses words that sound long and complicated – words he does not fully understand himself. To appreciate the effect of the text fully, it is important that you understand these words. However, if you are not sure, you should at least realise that these words are not necessarily being used correctly, but to scare the people reading the letters as they would not know the words.

Journey to Castle Dracula

Jonathan Harker is travelling alone through the Carpathian Mountains in Romania in a horse-drawn carriage driven by a mysterious coachman.

Soon we were hemmed in with trees, which in places arched right over the roadway till we passed as through a tunnel; and again great frowning rocks guarded us boldly on either side. Though we were in shelter, we could hear the rising wind, for it moaned and whistled through the rocks, and the branches of the trees crashed together as we swept along. It grew colder and colder still, and fine
5 powdery snow began to fall, so that soon we and all around us were covered with a white blanket. The keen wind still carried the howling of the dogs, though this grew fainter as we went on our way. The baying of the wolves sounded nearer and nearer, as though they were closing round on us from every side. I grew dreadfully afraid, and the horses shared my fear; but the driver was not in the least disturbed. He kept turning his head to left and right, but I could not see anything through the darkness.

10 Suddenly, away on our left, I saw a faint flickering blue flame. The driver saw it at the same moment; he at once checked the horses and, jumping to the ground, disappeared into the darkness. I did not know what to do, the less as the howling of the wolves drew closer; but while I wondered the driver suddenly appeared again, and without a word took his seat, and we resumed our journey. I think I must have fallen asleep and kept dreaming of the incident, for it seemed to be repeated endlessly, and now,
15 looking back, it is like a sort of awful nightmare. Once the flame appeared so near the road that even in the darkness around us I could watch the driver's motions. He went rapidly to where the blue flame rose – it must have been very faint, for it did not seem to illumine the place around it at all – and gathering a few stones, formed them into some device. Once there appeared a strange optical effect: when he stood between me and the flame he did not obstruct it for I could see its ghostly flicker all the same. This
20 startled me, but as the effect was only momentary, I took it that my eyes deceived me straining through the darkness. Then for a time there were no blue flames, and we sped onwards through the gloom, with the howling of the wolves around us, as though they were following in a moving circle.

At last there came a time when the driver went further afield than he had yet done, and during his absence the horses began to tremble worse than ever and to snort and scream with fright. I
25 could not see any cause for it, for the howling of the wolves had ceased altogether; but just then the moon, sailing through the black clouds, appeared behind the jagged crest of a beetling, pineclad rock, and by its light I saw around us a ring of wolves, with white teeth and lolling red tongues, with long, sinewy limbs and shaggy hair. They were a hundred times more terrible in the grim silence which held them than even when they howled. For myself, I felt a sort of paralysis of fear. It is only
30 when a man feels himself face to face with such horrors that he can understand their true import.

Read the passage entitled 'Journey to Castle Dracula' which is taken from Dracula *by Bram Stoker (first published in 1897) and answer the questions that follow at the appropriate level, using complete sentences.*

The marks given for each question are a guide as to how much you should write in your answers.

LEVEL 2 questions

1 (a) What mood does the author create in the first paragraph?   (1)

   (b) How does he create this mood?   (6)

2 What does the driver do when he spots a blue flame?   (3)

3 What clues in the text make you think the coachman might not be an
   ordinary human being?   (6)

4 In what way do the wolves add to the tension of the extract? Explain
   your opinion in detail, making reference to the text.   (6)

5 Comment briefly on the effectiveness of having a first person narrator in
   this passage.   (3)

LEVEL 1 questions

1   Look at lines 11–19. Describe what the driver does when he sees a
     blue flame.   (3)

2   (a)   The mood in the first paragraph (lines 1–10) is one of
            claustrophobia, of being closed in. Write down three quotations
            that help create this atmosphere.   (3)

     (b)   Choose two of these quotations and describe in as much detail as
            you can how they are effective.   (4)

3   (a)   There are a number of clues in the text that suggest that the driver
            is not an ordinary human being. Write down two quotations that
            make you think this.   (2)

     (b)   Explain your choices in detail.   (4)

4   (a)   Throughout the passage the wolves add to the tension. Note down
            three different ways in which the wolves scare the narrator in the extract. (3)

     (b)   For each incident, explain briefly in what way this creates tension. (3)

5   Do you think the story is more effective because it has a narrator who
     tells the story? Explain your thoughts briefly.   (3)

Notes on the text

You have probably heard of Dracula. The book by Bram Stoker is a work of fiction about a vampire. The introduction to the questions tells you the book was written in 1897, so at the end of the Victorian era and before modern technology.

The introduction makes it clear that the narrator is travelling in a horse-drawn carriage through Romania, so eastern mainland Europe. The driver who is mentioned frequently in the passage is therefore the coachman, the person guiding the carriage and horses. There are no cars or motors in this passage!

The passage is written from Harker's point of view and we share only his knowledge.

The passage is mainly atmospheric and draws its tension from the interplay of wolves howling, the horses' fright, Harker's uneasiness and the strange actions of the driver. Very little is stated definitely and we are left to guess what kind of person the driver is.

The first paragraph sets the scene for the night-time journey and includes all the elements that will crop up again later. Note the frequent use of onomatopoeia, which suits the description of travelling through darkness.

3 Poetry comprehensions

Introduction

This chapter contains five poetry comprehensions. It is designed to give you specific practice for Paper 2, Section A of the exam. The poems are all by twentieth century poets, reflecting the kind of poem examiners set for CE papers.

The exercises have been laid out to copy as closely as possible the presentation of poetry comprehensions in the actual exam so that you can familiarise yourself with the format. The text of the poem is followed by the Level 2 questions, as this is the level most pupils will be taking. The Level 1 questions are on the next page and it is a good idea to photocopy these, so if you are practising Level 1 you can also have the questions facing the text, as it would be in the exam.

The questions and marks all mirror current exam board practice.

After the questions is a short section on how to approach the poem and hints on how to decode its meaning. This will help you to practise decoding a poem by focusing your thoughts on what you should be thinking about while reading a poem.

When working through each comprehension bear in mind the following:
- You have about 35 minutes to complete each comprehension exercise, which includes reading and note-making time.
- You should answer all questions.
- Language, spelling, grammar, punctuation and presentation are important.

Stealing

The most unusual thing I ever stole? A snowman.
Midnight. He looked magnificent; a tall, white mute
beneath the winter moon. I wanted him, a mate
with a mind as cold as the slice of ice
5 within my own brain. I started with the head.

Better off dead than giving in, not taking
what you want. He weighed a ton; his torso,
frozen stiff, hugged to my chest, a fierce chill
piercing my gut. Part of the thrill was knowing
10 that children would cry in the morning. Life's tough.

Sometimes I steal things I don't need. I joy-ride cars
to nowhere, break into houses just to have a look.
I'm a mucky ghost, leave a mess, maybe pinch a camera.
I watch my gloved hand twisting the doorknob.
15 A stranger's bedroom. Mirrors. I sigh like this – Aah.

It took some time. Reassembled in the yard,
he didn't look the same. I took a run
and booted him. Again. Again. My breath ripped out
in rags. It seems daft now. Then I was standing
20 alone amongst lumps of snow, sick of the world.

Boredom. Mostly I'm so bored I could eat myself.
One time, I stole a guitar and thought I might
learn to play. I nicked a bust of Shakespeare once,
flogged it, but the snowman was strangest.
25 You don't understand a word I'm saying, do you?

      Carol Ann Duffy

Read the poem 'Stealing' by Carol Ann Duffy and answer the questions that follow at the appropriate level, using complete sentences.

The marks given for each question are a guide as to how much you should write in your answers.

LEVEL 2 questions

1   The poem starts and ends with a question. What effect does this have?   (3)

2   Why do you think the poet included the word 'Aah' in line 15?   (2)

3   What kind of language does the poet use? Write down two examples and explain in what way the language used is effective.   (4)

4   What do you think is the relevance of the guitar and the bust of Shakespeare?   (4)

5   Why do you think the narrator stole the snowman and why is he telling this story in particular? Refer closely to the poem to support your ideas.   (6)

6   How can you tell that the narrator does not share the values of society in general? You should write down and discuss three quotations to support your ideas.   (6)

LEVEL 1 questions

1   (a)   Why do you think the poem starts with a question?   (2)

     (b)   Why do you think the poem ends with another question?   (2)

2   The poet uses a lot of short phrases. Why might this be?   (4)

3   Name four things the narrator has stolen.   (4)

4   What makes the stealing of the snowman unusual? Give two reasons and explain them in detail, using the text to support your ideas.   (2+4)

5   The narrator is obviously someone who does not have the same values as everyone else. Find three quotations that show this.   (3)

6   How does the author make us believe this really is a thief talking?   (4)

Notes on the poem

The style of the poem is colloquial – this is meant to copy the way thief might speak. In fact, the poem is the record of what the person says; essentially a monologue. The sentences are mainly short and often jump from one topic to another. The poem doesn't really tell a story; it is a collection of thoughts.

In the poem the narrator tells all the things he has stolen and by so doing reveals his character. As the poem jumps from topic to topic, it is important that you realise what each stanza is about.

Stanza one describes the snowman and why the narrator decides to steal him.

Stanza two describes the deed.

Stanza three tells us of the other robberies and break-ins he has committed.

Stanza four returns to the snowman (the clue is the 'he' in line 17 and the fact that he's 'reassembled' – line 16).

Stanza five tells of other things he's stolen.

The poem is quite easy to understand. The slang should not pose any significant difficulties and can be guessed in most cases: to joy-ride cars is to drive in stolen cars; pinch and nick both mean steal and flog is to sell.

The main difficulty of the poem is understanding the mind of the thief.

What the poet is trying to get across is that the thief steals for no other reason than boredom and spite. It sounds like a young person talking, not only because of the slang, but also because the thefts do not sound professional, such as an adult would carry out. The poem is a sketch of the thief's character: someone who does not respect society or its laws, but makes his own, which do not satisfy him either, though.

The Thought-Fox

I imagine this midnight moment's forest:
Something else is alive
Beside the clock's loneliness
And this blank page where my fingers move.

5 Through the window I see no star:
Something more near
Though deeper within darkness
Is entering the loneliness:

Cold, delicately as the dark snow
10 A fox's nose touches twig, leaf;
Two eyes serve a movement, that now
And again now, and now, and now

Sets neat prints into the snow
Between trees, and warily a lame
15 Shadow lags by stump and in hollow
Of a body that is bold to come

Across clearings, an eye,
A widening deepening greenness,
Brilliantly, concentratedly,
20 Coming about its own business

Till, with a sudden sharp hot stink of fox
It enters the dark hole of the head.
The window is starless still; the clock ticks,
The page is printed.

      Ted Hughes

Read the poem 'The Thought-Fox' by Ted Hughes and answer the questions that follow at the appropriate level, using complete sentences.

The marks given for each question are a guide as to how much you should write in your answers.

LEVEL 2 questions

1   How does the poet make the night sound dreary? In your answer you
should use quotes briefly to support your points.   (6)

2   Explain line 12.   (4)

3   How can you tell that at the end of the poem something has changed in
the night?   (3)

4   How does the poet make the fox come to life in the reader's head? Use
short quotations from the poem to support your arguments.   (6)

5   Do you think the poet is writing about a real encounter with a fox,
or has he imagined it all? Refer closely to the poem to support your
arguments.   (6)

LEVEL 1 questions

1   Look at lines 1–8. Write down two quotations that show the night is
    dreary and explain the effect of each quotation in detail.   (2+4)

2   Look at lines 11–14, which describe how the fox moves through the
    snow. How does the poet bring these movements to life? Select three
    quotations and explain each one briefly.   (6)

3   What has happened to the page at the end of the poem that is different
    from what it was like before?   (2)

4   (a)   The poem is quite obviously about a fox. Find three quotations
          that describe the fox.   (3)

    (b)   Explain what the quotations you selected tell you about the fox.   (3)

5   Line 22 states 'It enters the dark hole of the head.' What do you think is
    meant by this line? Explain your ideas as fully as possible.   (5)

Notes on the poem

The title suggests this is a poem about a fox of the mind.

The first stanza sets the scene: the poet is imagining a forest at midnight, where something else is alive while he is writing.

In the second stanza something seems to be coming to the poet.

The next three stanzas describe the fox moving through the forest, for that is what seems to have come. The description is quite sketchy and not all sentences make sense; this does not matter, as long as you get a feel for the descriptions.

Make sure you don't stop at line endings, but at punctuation marks!

So, read: Cold, delicately as the dark snow, a fox's nose touches twig, leaf; two eyes serve a movement, that now and again now, and now, and now sets neat prints into the snow between trees, and warily a lame shadow lags by stump and in hollow of a body that is bold to come across clearings, an eye, a widening deepening greenness, brilliantly, concentratedly, coming about its own business.

The suggestion is that the fox enters the poet's head, which leads to the writing of the poem and the printing of the page – the poem in front of you.

So, the poem is less a poem about a fox and more a poem about the creative process: while staring at a night forest, the poet imagines what might be in it and thus, slowly, the fox creeps into his head, becoming ever clearer and more detailed, until it lands on the page, as a poem about writing a poem about a fox.

From 'War Music'

In this extract from a re-telling of the Trojan war, Patroclus, who is wearing Achilles' armour, is being attacked by the god Apollo.

Coming behind you through the dust you felt
– What was it? – felt Creation part, and then

APOLLO!

Who had been patient with you

5 Struck.

His hand came from the east,
And in his wrist lay all eternity;
And every atom of his mythic weight
Was poised between his fist and bent left leg.

10 Your eyes lurched out. Achilles' bonnet rang
Far and away beneath the cannon-bones of Trojan horses,
And you were footless ... staggering ... amazed ...
Whirled to the outskirts of the battlefield,
Between its clumps of dying, dying yourself,
15 Dazed by the brilliance in your eyes,
The noise – like weirs heard far away –
Dabbling your astounded fingers
In the vomit on your chest.

And many wounded Trojans lay and stared at you;
20 Propped themselves up and stared at you;
Feeling themselves as blest as you felt cursed.

All of them lay and stared;
And one, a hero boy called Thackta, cast.
His javelin went through your calves,
25 Not noticing the pain, and tried to crawl away.

Christopher Logue

Read the extract from the epic poem War Music *by Christopher Logue and answer the questions that follow at the appropriate level, using complete sentences.*

The marks given for each question are a guide as to how much you should write in your answers.

LEVEL 2 questions

1   Who is the narrator addressing in this extract?   (1)

2   In the original, lines 3 and 4 are on a separate double page, with the word 'Apollo!' spaced across the whole two pages. Why do you think the poet chose this layout?   (4)

3   How does the author make the wounding of Patroclus vivid? Refer closely to the text in your answer.   (8)

4   Explain the Trojans' reactions to the wounds of Patroclus.   (6)

5   The extract is quite graphic in its description of violence. Do you think this is a valid topic and style for poetry? Explain your point of view, referring to the text where necessary.   (6)

LEVEL 1 questions

1   In the poem the poet keeps referring to 'you' as though he was addressing someone. Who is this 'you' the poet is pretending to talk to?   (1)

2   Why do you think the poet has written the single word Apollo in capital letters across the whole page?   (4)

3   (a)   The wounding of Patroclus is described in great detail in lines 5–18. Select three quotations you find particularly effective.   (3)

   (b)   For each quotation selected, explain your choice in detail.   (6)

4   (a)   Select three words that describe how the Trojans react to the wounding of Patroclus in lines 19–23.   (3)

   (b)   Explain briefly what your choices tell us about the Trojans.   (3)

5   Do you think that such a description of a battle makes a good poem? Refer to the text where necessary to support your views.   (5)

Notes on the poem

If you know of the Trojan War, then you will probably find this extract easier to understand.

The first thing you should realise is that the 'you' is Patroclus and the 'he' is Apollo.

Lines 6–9 describe Apollo's striking of Patroclus.

Lines 10–18 are Patroclus's reaction to being wounded.

'Bonnet' is a weird word in the context, but it is clear that it must mean the helmet.

'the cannon-bones of Trojan horses' might not be altogether clear, but the general sense and gist (bones of horses on the battlefield) should be.

Remember that Patroclus has been struck by a god ('the brilliance in your eyes' – line 15), so it is possible that he is literally 'whirled to the outskirts of the battlefield'.

Lines 19–21 describe the reaction of the Trojans.

'cast' in line 23 means to throw.

This is an extract from a longer narrative poem that retells the Trojan War. It has no specific meaning or message beyond the story, but it is a detailed look at dying and also tries to bring across the sudden appearance of a god and how it might affect humans.

Eden Rock

They are waiting for me somewhere beyond Eden Rock:
My father, twenty-five, in the same suit
Of Genuine Irish Tweed, his terrier Jack
Still two years old and trembling at his feet.

5 My mother, twenty-three, in a *sprigged dress
Drawn at the waist, ribbon in her straw hat,
Has spread the stiff white cloth over the grass.
Her hair, the colour of wheat, takes on the light.

She pours tea from a Thermos, the milk straight
10 From an old H.P. sauce bottle, a screw
Of paper for a cork; slowly sets out
The same three plates, the tin cups painted blue.

The sky whitens as if lit by three suns.
My mother shades her eyes and looks my way
15 Over the drifted stream. My father spins
A stone along the water. Leisurely,

They beckon to me from the other bank.
I hear them call, 'See where the stream-path is!
Crossing is not as hard as you might think.'

20 I had not thought that it would be like this.

      Charles Causley

Glossary

*sprigged – decorated with small stems bearing leaves or flowers

Read the poem 'Eden Rock' by Charles Causley and answer the questions that follow at the appropriate level, using complete sentences.

The marks given for each question are a guide as to how much you should write in your answers.

LEVEL 2 questions

1   How can you tell that in describing the scene the poet sees
'somewhere beyond Eden Rock' he is recalling a memory? Refer to the
text in your answer.   (6)

2   Explain the significance of line 13, 'My mother shades her eyes and
looks my way'.   (4)

3   The fourth stanza introduces the image of a river. What do you think
the river represents in the poem? Refer closely to the poem in your answer.   (6)

4   The poem ends with the line 'I had not thought that it would be like
this.' What is the poet referring to? Use short quotations from the poem
to support your arguments.   (6)

5   What does the title 'Eden Rock' suggest to you? Why do you think the
poet chose this title?   (3)

LEVEL 1 questions

1   What does the word 'Eden' in the title make you think of?   (3)

2   In lines 2–11 the poet is describing a memory.

    (a)   Write down two quotations that tell you that time has stood still.   (2)

    (b)   Explain your choices in detail.   (4)

3   In stanza 4 (lines 13–16) the action changes. Describe what is going on in these lines.   (4)

4   Lines 17–20 are about crossing a stream.

    (a)   Find two quotations that tell you something about this crossing.   (2)

    (b)   Explain your choices and what they tell you about crossing.   (4)

5   What do you think the poem is really about? Explain your ideas, referring to the text where necessary.   (6)

Notes on the poem

The colon at the end of line 1 means the following lines will explain who 'they' are.

The first two stanzas are very straightforward and contain very clear and simple descriptions of the father, the dog and the mother.

Remember once again to read to the punctuation.

Note the words 'same' (line 2) and 'still' (line 4) as well as the age of the parents: these are not realistic ages for parents of someone writing the poem. Either the narrator is a baby or this is not a real scene, but a memory or a photo.

The third stanza describes the picnic.

With the fourth stanza things start to get strange, though the words are still readily understandable. For some reason the sky whitens and the parents are suddenly on the other side of a stream, asking the narrator to cross.

The meaning of the poem depends very much on what you make of these last eight lines. Remember they must make sense when read together with the beginning.

The suggestion is that this is a memory of a truly happy moment that the narrator recalls now that he is about to cross over. This crossing over can be growing up, suggesting the narrator does not want to follow his parents into adulthood, which they find easy ('leisurely'), but he obviously doesn't. The fact that he can't find the stream-path suggests he doesn't know how to grow older correctly, either. The crossing over can also be dying. His parents are trying to help him to make the journey into the afterlife, an afterlife that is not difficult: an unexpected vision of death as the last line attests this.

A Boy in Church

'Gabble-gabble … brethren … gabble-gabble!'
      My window glimpses larch and heather.
I hardly hear the tuneful babble,
      Not knowing nor much caring whether
5 The text is praise or exhortation,
   Prayer or thanksgiving or damnation.

Outside it blows wetter and wetter,
      The tossing trees never stay still;
I shift my elbows to catch better
10   The full round sweep of heathered hill.
   The tortured copse bends to and fro
   In silence like a shadow-show.

The parson's voice runs like a river
      Over smooth rock. I like this church.
15 The pews are staid, they never shiver,
      They never bend or sway or lurch.
   'Prayer,' says the kind voice, 'is a chain
   That draws Grace down from heaven again.'

I add the hymns up over and over
20   Until there's not the least mistake.
   Seven-seventy-one. (Look! There's a plover!
      It's gone!) Who's that Saint by the Lake?
   The red light from his mantle passes
   Across the broad memorial brasses.

25 It's pleasant here for dreams and thinking,
      Lolling and letting reason nod,
   With ugly, serious people thinking
      Prayer-chains for a forgiving God.
   But a dumb blast sets the trees swaying
30 With furious zeal like madmen praying.

      Robert Graves

Read the poem 'A Boy in Church' by Robert Graves and answer the questions that follow at the appropriate level, using complete sentences.

The marks given for each question are a guide as to how much you should write in your answers.

LEVEL 2 questions

1 What is happening inside the church and what outside? (2)

2 How can you tell the boy is bored? You should discuss short quotations in your answer. (6)

3 How does rhyme add to the effect of the poem? (4)

4 How does the poet bring the scene outside the church to life? (6)

5 (a) What do the last two lines suggest? (1)

(b) In what way are the trees, the people praying and the boy linked? (6)

1 (a) What is happening inside the church?   (2)

   (b) What is happening outside the church?   (2)

2 (a) Write down two quotations that tell you the boy is bored.   (2)

   (b) Explain your choices in detail.   (4)

3 (a) The stanzas of the poem are regular: they are all built the same
      way. Write down which lines in each stanza rhyme.   (3)

   (b) In what way does the rhyme support what the poem is saying?   (2)

4 Write down two quotations about the storm outside that you find
  effective and explain what they tell you.   (2+4)

5 Look carefully at the last two lines and at the whole poem again. In
  what way are the people praying and the trees similar? Use quotations
  to support your points where you can.   (4)

Notes on the poem

The title is important here, as it tells you exactly what the poem is about.

A basic knowledge of Christian Mass or church service is helpful to fully understand this poem.

The poem starts with direct speech that mirrors what is said in church ('brethren' is a word typically used in church only). The next line takes us to the scenery that can be seen from the church window.

This is the basic structure throughout the poem: what goes on in the church and outside.

The first stanza continues to describe the words being said and the boy's indifference to what they are or mean.

Stanza two takes us out of the church.

'copse' is a small wood.

The third stanza is inside again.

'staid' is respectable and unadventurous. The pews (made of wood) are being compared to the trees outside.

The fourth stanza describes what the boy does in his boredom and the different things his roving eyes see.

The last stanza sums up the boy's experience and contrasts it with the praying of the other people, which is related to the trees.

The poem, superficially about a boy bored in church; it is more deeply, about praying and how the trees also seem to pray. The message seems to be that when hit by storms, you start to pray. So, while the boy might be bored now, the suggestion is that later, when hit by the blows of life, he might start praying, too.

4 Prose for a purpose

Introduction

This chapter presents a number of titles designed as specific practice for Paper 1, Section B of the exam. This section of the exam is entirely new and asks you to use writing to achieve a certain purpose. Of the different kinds of possibilities, the exam board syllabus mentions writing to argue, persuade, explain, advise or inform. Consequently, titles have been grouped into these categories, with one mixed section at the end.

Your writing in any of these genres could be in the form of a letter, a speech or a newspaper article, as well as a simple essay. The questions invite you to explore a number of these different writing types.

When working through each task bear in mind the following:
- You have about 40 minutes to complete each writing task, which includes time for choosing your title and planning.
- You should answer only one question.
- Language, spelling, grammar, punctuation and presentation are important.
- Credit will also be given for effective use of language.

Writing to argue

1   Our technology is becoming so advanced and powerful that very soon we will have no need of nature. Do you agree? Write an essay in which you argue either for or against this proposition.

2   Family is more important than friends. Discuss this statement.

3   To be able to compete with Asia and China, schools should be academic hothouses, focusing on providing high-quality lessons only. Games and other non-academic activities should be carried out after school, for those who want to do them. Write a balanced essay that looks at both sides of the issue.

Writing to persuade

1   Write a letter to the governing body of your school in which you argue that the top year group should have an educational trip to London lasting a few days.

2   Write an article for your school magazine in which you make a case for pupils being allowed to wear jewellery and other adornments in school.

3   Write a persuasive piece in which you argue that your school should have a vending machine selling sweets and fizzy drinks.

Writing to explain

1   Explain your favourite computer game to a novice. Remember to state what kind of game it is, what the objective is and what you have to do to progress through the game.

2   Why is science important? Write a speech to be delivered at your school's science fair in which you answer this question in a factual style.

3   Explain what kind of a person you have to be to become a school prefect. In your answer you might want to focus on characteristics, attitude and behaviour.

Writing to advise

1   Imagine you are giving a fellow pupil advice on what kind of senior school to go to. Remember to shape your advice to the age of the pupil you are writing for.

2   You have been asked to write a pamphlet informing pupils which sports they can take up. You should present each sport briefly, its pros and cons and then give a short evaluation.

3   A pupil has come to you for advice on social networking. The pupil uses the internet, but has not yet had any experience of social networking sites and would like your help.

Writing to inform

1   Write an article for the local newspaper in which you state what to look out for when acquiring a new smartphone.

2   Write about a moment when you weren't strong enough.

3   What is your favourite holiday destination? Write your piece in such a way that it becomes clear why you like the place so much.

Mixed

1   Write an article for your school newspaper's 'Agony Aunt' column, in which you tell someone what to wear to the school disco.

2   Two's company, three's a crowd. Do you prefer being alone or with many people? Explain your point of view.

3   The way to school usually goes unnoticed. What is your journey to school like? Describe it in a way that lets the reader share the journey.

4   Write a letter to your local MP persuading him to introduce a ban on keeping exotic pets (like snakes, lizards or lions).

5 Writing about books

Introduction

Paper 1, Section B contains two different types of writing task: the first three questions ask you to use prose for a purpose (for which practice can be found in the previous chapter) and the fourth question asks you to write about books. This chapter provides a number of tasks so that you can practise this genre of writing.

Central to this type of writing is the use of a book to support your arguments. The questions are not geared towards any specific book, but are general in nature. Most will ask you to examine moments of drama, transition, contrast or other important moments in your reading. Which books you use is up to you. You can write about one or more.

When working through each task bear in mind the following:

- You have about 40 minutes to complete each writing task, which includes time for choosing your title and planning.
- You should answer only one question.
- Vocabulary, spelling, grammar, punctuation and presentation are important.
- Credit will be given for effective use of language.

Practice titles

1 A good book is a friend for life. Discuss this statement, using your own reading to support your arguments.

2 In the past and in many places now authorities ban or burn books they deem dangerous. Do you think books can be dangerous? Explain your point of view, using one or more books you have read as examples.

3 Really interesting books do not have 'goodies' and 'baddies', but more developed and subtle characters. Have you found this to be true in your reading?

4 'Rather than read a book, you should go out and live life.'
'One book contains a hundred lives.'
Discuss these two opposing views, using books you have read to support your arguments.

5 The first few paragraphs usually give you a good idea of what a book will be like. Write about a book that surprised you, where the book turned out to be completely different from what the first few paragraphs suggested.

6 A good book will keep you awake. Have you ever read a book that you just couldn't put down? Write about it, explaining what made the book so memorable and exciting.

7 You can tell what kind of a person someone is by the books she or he is reading. Explain, based on two or more books you have read, what kind of a person they show you to be, and why.

8 Endings are always difficult and most book endings are unsatisfactory. Discuss this statement using your own reading to support your arguments.

9 Good books need to be shared. Have you found this to be true? In your answer use one or more books you have read to support your point of view.

10 'It doesn't matter how well a book is written as long as the story is good.' What is more important: style or plot? Answer this question, using one or more books you have read as examples.

6 Creative writing

Introduction

Creative writing is the final section of the exam (Paper 2, Section B). In it you are asked to write descriptive or narrative pieces that are either based on reality or are entirely fictional or fantastical. Which you do is entirely up to you.

This chapter contains a number of different titles of the kind you could receive in the exam. Some of the questions give you more guidance and some give you a phrase to include in the story; others are merely a title.

When working through each task bear in mind the following:

- You have about 40 minutes to complete each writing task, which includes time for choosing your title and planning.
- You should answer only one question.
- Vocabulary, spelling, grammar, punctuation and presentation are important.
- Credit will also be given for imaginative and exciting writing.

Practice titles

1   Describe a morning that was particularly memorable.

2   Describe a building that impressed you. You might want to include the surroundings of the building or what goes on inside, as well as your reaction to it.

3   Describe a moment of intense concentration, when you focused so hard you forgot the world around you.

4   Describe a person you admire; this can be an historical person or someone living now. Remember to include in your description why you look up to that person.

5   'The early bird catches the worm.'
    Describe a situation in which you were quick off the mark and won 'the worm'.

6   'I never have any luck.'
    Write a story that includes this sentence.

7   'Now we're stuck!'
    Write a story that includes someone saying these words.

8   Write a story that either begins or ends with the following words:
    'The only person to blame is me.'

9   Write a story that includes the following words:
    'Darkness fell as suddenly as a guillotine.'

10 'She never found her way home again.'
    Write a story that includes this sentence.

11 In the Thick of Things

12 A Spire

13 The Fountain at the End of the World

14 Hungry Heart

15 The Confidence Trickster

16 The Dark Side of the Moon

17 Let Me In

18 Gone Too Long

19 Suburbia

20 Beyond Time

7 Practice papers

This section contains five full mock Common Entrance papers, looking much like those you will receive in the actual exam. The order is the same as in the exam and a layout has been selected that works optimally for Level 2 candidates, with comprehension questions facing the text. Level 1 candidates should photocopy their questions, so that they, too, have text and questions facing each other.

General information on the exam:

- You have 1 hour 15 minutes for each paper. This includes time for reading the passages, taking notes and planning.
- In each paper, answer all the questions in Section A, but only one question from Section B.
- Technical accuracy (spelling, grammar and punctuation), word choice, as well as presentation, are all important and will be taken into account.

Practice paper 1

Bringing the Cows In

James Herriot is a vet in Yorkshire who also inspects cows for the Government. For him to be able to check the cows, they have to be in their shed. Mr Kay's heifers (cows) in this extract have so far refused to co-operate in any way and are still not in the shed.

'Aye, it's no good,' he said. 'We'll have to get Sam.'

'Sam?'

'Aye, Sam Broadbent. He'll get 'em in all right.'

'How's he going to do that?'

5 'Oh, he can imitate a fly.'

For a moment my mind reeled. 'Did you say imitate a fly?'

'That's right. A warble fly; tha knows. He's a bit slow is t'lad but by gaw he can imitate a fly. I'll go and get him – he's only two fields down the road.'

I watched the farmer's retreating back in disbelief then threw myself down on the ground. My
10 mind was a turmoil. I had a full day's Ministry work waiting for me and I was an hour behind time already. I could picture the long succession of farmers waiting for me and cursing me heartily. The tension built in me till I could stand it no longer; I jumped to my feet and ran down to the gate at the foot. I could see along the road from there and was relieved to find that Mr Kay was on his way back.

Just behind him a large, fat man was riding slowly on a very small bicycle, his heels on the
15 pedals, his feet and knees sticking out at right angles. Tufts of greasy black hair stuck out at random from under a kind of skull cap which looked like an old bowler without the brim.

'Sam's come to give us a hand,' said Mr Kay.

'Good morning,' I said and the big man turned slowly and nodded. The eyes in the round, unshaven face were vacant and incurious and I decided that Sam did indeed look a bit slow. I found
20 it difficult to imagine how he could possibly be of any help.

The heifers, standing near by, watched with languid interest as we came through the gate. They had obviously enjoyed every minute of the morning's entertainment and it seemed they were game for a little more fun if we so desired; but it was up to us, of course – they weren't worried either way.

Sam propped his bicycle against the wall and paced solemnly forward. He made a circle of
25 his thumb and forefinger and placed it to his lips. His cheeks worked as though he was getting everything into place, then he took a deep breath. And from nowhere it seemed came a sudden swelling of angry sound, a vicious humming and buzzing which made me look round in alarm for the enraged insect zooming in for the kill.

The effect on the heifers was electric. Their superior air vanished and was replaced by rigid
30 anxiety; then, as the noise increased in volume, they turned and charged up the hill. But it wasn't the carefree frolic of before – no tossing heads, waving tails and kicking heels; this time they kept shoulder to shoulder in a frightened block.

Mr Kay and I, trotting on either side, directed them yet again up to the building where they formed a group, looking nervously around them.

35 We had to wait for a short while for Sam to arrive. He was clearly a one-pace man and ascended the slope unhurriedly. At the top he paused to regain his breath, fixed the animals with a blank gaze and carefully adjusted his fingers against his mouth. A moment's tense silence then the humming broke out again, even more furious and insistent than before.

(abridged)

Read the passage entitled 'Bringing the Cows In' which is taken from All Creatures Great and Small *by James Herriot and answer the questions that follow at the appropriate level, using complete sentences.*

The marks given for each question are a guide as to how much you should write in your answers.

LEVEL 2 questions

1   Why does Herriot throw himself down on the ground (line 9)? Explain
     your answer in as much detail as you can.   (4)

2   In your own words describe the first appearance of Sam Broadbent.   (4)

3   How does Herriot make Sam's humming effective? In your answer you
     should refer closely to the text.   (6)

4   The passage is written in a humorous fashion. Find three quotations
     that you think are funny and explain how they achieve their effect.   (6)

5   What kind of a person do you think Sam is? Write down two quotations
     that tell you something about him and explain your ideas in as much
     detail as possible.   (5)

LEVEL 1 questions

1   Give two reasons why Herriot throws himself down on the ground in line 9.   (4)

2   Look at lines 14–20. Describe Sam Broadbent using your own words as much as possible.   (5)

3   Look at lines 24–38.

      (a)   Note down two quotations that make the description of Sam's humming come to life.   (2)

      (b)   Explain your choices in detail.   (4)

4   (a)   Write down three quotations that you think are funny.   (3)

      (b)   Explain your choices briefly.   (3)

5   What kind of a person is Sam? Write down two characteristics and for each one find a quotation that shows it.   (4)

Paper 1, Section B: Writing task

BOTH LEVELS

Write on any ONE of the following topics. Each one is worth 25 marks.

Credit will be given for good spelling, punctuation and presentation, as well as for appropriate use of style and language.

1   Do you prefer to travel by plane, train or automobile? Write about an actual trip by one of these means of transport, stating what was so good about it.

2   'It is more important that children are loved than that they are challenged.' Discuss this statement, highlighting both sides of the issue and using examples wherever possible.

3   Write advice for your school magazine on how best to prepare for exams.

4   EITHER

   (a)   Do you prefer books in which the hero has some special powers, like Harry Potter or Percy Jackson, or those in which the main character is an ordinary human being?

   OR

   (b)   'Some books are to be tasted, others to be swallowed, and some few to be chewed and digested.' (Francis Bacon)
   Have you had a similar reading experience? Write about a book or books you have either only tasted, swallowed down or chewed carefully, explaining what made you do so.

Death of a Gardener

He rested through the winter, watched the rain
On his cold garden, slept, awoke to snow
Padding the window, thatching the roof again
With silence. He was grateful for the slow
5 Nights and undemanding days; the dark
Protected him; the pause grew big with cold.
Mice in the shed scuffled like leaves; a spark
Hissed from his pipe as he dreamed beside the fire

All at once light sharpened; earth drew breath,
10 Stirred; and he woke to strangeness that was spring,
Stood on the grass, felt movement underneath
Like a child in the womb; hope troubled him to bring
Barrow and spade once more to the waiting soil.
Slower his lift and thrust; a blackbird filled
15 Long intervals with song; a worm could coil
To safety underneath the hesitant blade.
Hands tremulous as cherry branches kept
Faith with struggling seedlings till the earth
Kept faith with him, claimed him as he slept
20 Cold in the sun beside his guardian spade.

     Phoebe Hesketh

Read the poem 'Death of a Gardener' by Phoebe Hesketh and answer the questions that follow at the appropriate level, using complete sentences.

The marks given for each question are a guide as to how much you should write in your answers.

LEVEL 2 questions

1   What does the gardener do during the winter?   (2)

2   What do we learn about the winter in the first stanza? Use quotations
    from the text to support your view.   (6)

3   How does the poet make the seasons come to life?   (6)

4   What makes it clear in the second stanza that the gardener is getting
    old and weary?   (6)

5   Do you have the impression that the gardener's death was an easy
    one? Explain your view in detail, using quotations where appropriate.   (5)

1   (a)   Look at lines 1, 2 and 8. Write down three things that the gardener does during the winter. (3)

     (b)   Look at lines 10–13. Write down two things that the gardener does when spring arrives. (2)

2   Look at the first stanza (lines 1–8). What do we learn about the winter in these lines? You should use short quotations to support your ideas. (4)

3   Onomatopoeia is when a word sounds like what it is describing.

     (a)   Look at the first stanza. Find two examples of onomatopoeia. (2)

     (b)   Explain how the words make the description of winter vivid. (4)

4   (a)   Write down two quotations from lines 14–18 that tell us that the gardener is getting old and tired. (2)

     (b)   Explain your choices. (4)

5   The poet wants us to think that the gardener's death was an easy one. Write down two quotations from the last four lines which indicate an easy death. (lines 17–20). (4)

BOTH LEVELS

Write on any ONE of the following topics. Each one is worth 25 marks.

Credit will be given for good spelling, punctuation and presentation, as well as for imaginative and exciting use of language.

1   Heavy Snow

2   In Sickness and in Health

3   Write a story or description using one of the following titles:
   - Someone Missing
   - Way Out Left
   - Never Alone

4   Write a story that begins or ends with the following sentence: 'No one will ever know.'

Practice paper 2

Paper 1, Section A: Literary prose comprehension

Barn Dance

John Grady and Rawlins are two teenagers from Texas who rode to Mexico and are now working on a horse ranch there.

Although the night was cool the double doors of the grange stood open and the man selling the tickets was seated in a chair on a raised wooden platform just within the doors so that he must lean down to each in a gesture akin to benevolence and take their coins and hand them down their tickets or pass upon the ticketstubs of those who were only returning from outside. The old adobe hall was
5 buttressed along its outer walls with piers not all of which had been a part of its design and there were no windows and the walls were swagged and cracked. A string of electric bulbs ran the length of the hall at either side and the bulbs were covered with paper bags that had been painted and the brush strokes showed through in the light and the reds and greens and blues were all muted and much of a piece. The floor was swept but there were pockets of seeds underfoot and drifts of straw
10 and at the far end of the hall a small orchestra labored on a stage of grainpallets under a bandshell rigged from sheeting. Along the foot of the stage were lights set in fruitcans among colored crepe that smoldered throughout the night. The mouths of the cans were lensed with tinted cellophane and they cast upon the sheeting a shadowplay in the lights and smoke of antic demon players and a pair of *goathawks arced chittering through the partial darkness overhead.

15   John Grady and Rawlins and a boy named Roberto from the ranch stood just beyond the reach of light at the door among the cars and wagons and passed among themselves a pint medicine-bottle of *mescal. Roberto held the bottle to the light.

     *A las chicas, he said.

     He drank and handed off the bottle. They drank. They poured salt from a paper onto their
20 wrists and licked it off and Roberto pushed the cob stopper into the neck of the bottle and hid the bottle behind the tire of a parked truck and they passed around a pack of chewing gum.

     *Listos? he said.

     Listos.

     She was dancing with a tall boy from the San Pablo ranch and she wore a blue dress and her
25 mouth was red. He and Rawlins and Roberto stood with other youths along the wall and watched the dancers and watched beyond the dancers the young girls at the far side of the hall. He moved along past the groups. The air smelled of straw and sweat and a rich spice of colognes. Under the bandshell the accordion player struggled with his instrument and slammed his boot on the boards in countertime and stepped back and the trumpet player came forward. Her eyes above the shoulder of
30 her partner swept across him where he stood. Her black hair done up in a blue ribbon and the nape of her neck pale as porcelain. When she turned again she smiled.

     He'd never touched her and her hand was small and her waist so slight and she looked at him with great forthrightness and smiled and put her face against his shoulder. They turned under the lights. A long trumpet note guided the dancers on their separate and collective paths. Moths circled
35 the paper lights aloft and the goathawks passed down the wires and flared and arced upward into the darkness again.

Glossary

***mescal** – a type of Mexican alcohol
***A las chicas** – to the girls
***listos** – ready
***goathawk** – a type of hawk

Read the passage entitled 'Barn Dance' which is taken from All the Pretty Horses by Cormac McCarthy and answer the questions that follow at the appropriate level, using complete sentences.

The marks given for each question are a guide as to how much you should write in your answers.

LEVEL 2 questions

1   How have the people decorated the grange to make it look more festive for the barn dance?   (4)

2   How does the author bring the barn dance to life in lines 24–31?   (8)

3   (a)   Describe the ritual the boys perform before going in to the grange.   (2)

        (b)   Why do you think they do this?   (1)

4   Comment on the author's use of sentence structure.   (4)

5   What can you infer about the relationship between John Grady and the girl from the last two paragraphs? Use quotations from the text to support your arguments.   (6)

LEVEL 1 questions

1   Describe briefly what has been done to the grange to prepare it for the
    barn dance.   (4)

2   (a)   How does the author bring the barn dance to life in lines 24–31?   (3)

    (b)   Explain your choices in detail.   (6)

3   (a)   What do the boys do before entering the barn?   (2)

    (b)   Why do you think they do this?   (2)

4   The author sometimes uses very long sentences and then very short
    ones. Why do you think he has done this?   (2)

5   Look at lines 24–36. These are written from John Grady's point of view.

    (a)   Note down three quotations from these lines that tell you that
          John Grady and the girl are obviously interested in one another.   (3)

    (b)   Briefly explain your choices.   (3)

Paper 1, Section B: Writing task

BOTH LEVELS

Write on any ONE of the following topics. Each one is worth 25 marks.

Credit will be given for good spelling, punctuation and presentation, as well as for appropriate use of style and language.

1   Write an information leaflet that could be used in your school telling pupils about bullying and how to deal with it.

2   Telling the truth is, in the long run, always better than lying. Do you agree? Write an essay in which you explain your view.

3   'A friend in need is a friend indeed'. Write about a time when someone helped you, though you didn't expect it. Try to bring your experience to life as much as possible.

4   EITHER

    (a)   Most books for children and young adults nowadays come in series. Do you prefer to read series or separate books? In your answer you should refer to one or more books you have read.

    OR

    (b)   'The proper study of mankind is books.' (Aldous Huxley) What have you learnt about mankind from books that you have read?

Legs

Of well-fed babies activate
Digestive juices, yet I'm no cannibal.
It is my metaphysical teeth that wait
Impatiently to prove those goodies edible.
5 The pink or creamy bonelessness, as soft
As dough or mashed potato, does not show
A hint of how each pair of limbs will grow.
Schoolboys' are badged with scabs and starred with scars,
Their sisters', in white ankle-socks, possess
10 No calves as yet. They will, and when they do
Another kind of hunger will distress
Quite painfully, but pleasurably too.
Those lovely double stalks of girls give me
So much delight: the brown expensive ones,
15 Like fine twin creatures of rare pedigree,
Seem independent of their owners, so
Much themselves are they. Even the plain
Or downright ugly, the veined and cruelly blotched
That look like marble badly stained, I've watched
20 With pity and revulsion, yet something more –
A wonder at the variousness of things
Which share a name: the podgy oatmeal knees
Beneath the kilt, the muscled double weapons above boots,
Eloquence of dancers', suffering of *chars'
25 The wiry goatish, the long and smooth as milk –
O human legs, whose strangeness I sing,
You more than please, though pleasure you have brought me,
And there are often times when you transport me.

> (slightly abridged)

> Vernon Scannell

Glossary

*char (short for charwoman) – a cleaning lady

Read the extract from the poem 'Legs' by Vernon Scannell and answer the questions that follow at the appropriate level, using complete sentences.

The marks given for each question are a guide as to how much you should write in your answers.

LEVEL 2 questions

1   What are the first three kinds of leg that Scannell mentions?   (3)

2   How does the author make the description of the various kinds of leg
     effective?   (8)

3   Select two different types of leg that the poet describes and explain
     what he is telling us about them.   (4)

4   Comment on how rhythm and rhyme help to make the poem effective.   (6)

5   Look at the last three lines. Explain in your own words and with
     reference to the text, where appropriate, what you think the author means.   (4)

1   To whom do the first two kinds of leg that the poet mentions belong
    (lines 1–18)?   (4)

2   A simile is a comparison using 'as' or 'like'.

    (a)   Write down two examples of similes from the poem.   (2)

    (b)   Explain in detail how these similes are effective.   (4)

3   Select three different types of leg that the poet describes and explain in
    your own words what he is telling us about them.   (6)

4   (a)   The poem has quite a regular rhythm. Explain how this contributes
          to the effectiveness of the poem.   (2)

    (b)   The poem rhymes, but not regularly. Comment on how the rhymes
          make the poem come to life.   (2)

5   Look at the last three lines. What do you think the poet means?   (5)

Paper 2, Section B: Writing task

BOTH LEVELS

Write on any ONE of the following topics. Each one is worth 25 marks.

Credit will be given for good spelling, punctuation and presentation, as well as for imaginative and exciting use of language.

1   Getting Away From It All.

2   Write a descriptive piece using one of the following titles:
    - Autumn Leaves
    - Waves
    - The Mountain

3   Write a story that includes the following words: 'The man continued playing the accordion.'

4   Toeing the Line.

Practice paper 3

Vienna

Bill Bryson is travelling through Austria by train from Salzburg to Vienna, the next stop on his trip around Europe.

There is this curiously durable myth that European trains are wonderfully swift and smooth and a dream to travel on. The trains in Europe are in fact often tediously slow and for the most part the railways persist in the antiquated system of dividing the carriages into compartments. I used to think this was rather jolly and friendly, but you soon discover that it is like spending seven hours in a

5 waiting-room waiting for a doctor who never arrives. You are forced into an awkward intimacy with strangers, which I always find unsettling. If you do anything at all – take something from your pocket, stifle a yawn, rummage in your rucksack – everyone looks over to see what you're up to. There is no scope for privacy and of course there is nothing like being trapped in a train compartment on a long journey to bring all those unassuageable little frailties of the human body crowding to the front of

10 your mind.

I knew within minutes that I was going to like Vienna.

I went first to the cathedral. It is very grand and Gothic outside, but inside I found it oddly lifeless – the sort of place that gives you a cold shiver – and rather neglected as well. The brass was dull and unpolished, the pews were worn, the marble seemed heavy and dead, as if all the natural

15 luminescence had been drained from it. It was a relief to step back outside.

I went to a nearby Konditorei for coffee and a 15,000-calorie slice of cake and planned my assault on the city.

On the whole, the cafés were the biggest disappointment of Vienna to me. I've reached the time of life where my idea of a fabulous time is to sit around for half a day with a cup of coffee and a

20 newspaper, so a city teeming with coffee houses seemed made for me. I had expected them to be more special, full of smoky charm and eccentric characters, but they were just restaurants really. The coffee was OK, but not sensational, and the service was generally slow and always unfriendly. They provide you with newspapers, but so what? I can provide newspapers.

The one friendly café I found was the Hawelka, around the corner from my hotel. It was an

25 extraordinary place, musty, dishevelled and so dark that I had to feel my way to a table. Lying everywhere were newspapers on racks like carpet beaters. An old boy who was dressed more like a house painter than a waiter brought me a cup of coffee without asking if I wanted one and, upon recalling I was an American, began gathering up copies of USA Today.

'Oh no, please,' I said as he presented me with half a dozen. 'Put these on the fire and bring

30 me some newspapers.' But I don't think his hearing was good, and he scuttled around the room collecting even more and piling them on the table. 'No, no,' I protested; 'these are for lining drawers.' But he kept bringing them until I had a stack two feet high. He even opened one up and fixed it in front of me, so I drank my coffee and spent half an hour reading features about Vanna White, Sylvester Stallone and other great thinkers of our age.

(abridged)

Read the passage entitled 'Vienna', which is taken from Neither Here Nor There *by Bill Bryson and answer the questions that follow at the appropriate level, using complete sentences.*

The marks given for each question are a guide as to how much you should write in your answer.

LEVEL 2 questions

1   What does Bryson dislike about European trains?   (4)

2   How does Bryson bring his visit to the cathedral to life?   (6)

3   (a)   What does Bryson dislike about the Viennese cafés?   (3)

    (b)   What does he like about the Hawelka?   (3)

4   How does the author make the episode with USA Today funny?
    You should write down and discuss short quotations from the text in
    your answer.   (4)

5   Having read the extract, would you like to visit Vienna? Explain your
    reasons, referring to the passage where appropriate.   (5)

LEVEL 1 questions

1   Look at lines 1–10. What does Bryson dislike about European trains?   (4)

2   Look at lines 12–15.

   (a)   Write down two quotations that you think are effective in Bryson's description of the cathedral.   (2)

   (b)   Explain your choices in detail.   (4)

3   (a)   What does Bryson dislike about the Viennese cafés?   (3)

   (b)   What does he like about the Hawelka?   (3)

4   The little story at the end of the extract involving USA Today (lines 28–34) is meant to be funny. Write down two quotations that you think are humorous and explain your choice briefly.   (2+2)

5   Based on this extract, would you like to visit Vienna? Explain your reasons, using the text where necessary.   (5)

Paper 1, Section B: Writing task

BOTH LEVELS

Write on any ONE of the following topics. Each one is worth 25 marks.

Credit will be given for good spelling, punctuation and presentation, as well as for effective use of language and sentence structure.

1   Write an article for your school magazine in which you try to persuade the headteacher that you should be allowed to bring in pets to school.

2   Children are not very interested in politics. Write a letter to your local MP in which you outline what she or he could do to make politics more interesting and relevant for children and teenagers.

3   Sometimes you need to be alone. Write about a time when you felt this need, making sure you describe your experiences as clearly as possible.

4   EITHER

   (a)   'There are no new storylines.' Do you agree? In your answer you should refer to one or more books you have read.

   OR

   (b)   'Books are made like pyramids and they're just as useless!'
         (Gustave Flaubert)
         Write about a book that you have read that was either very useless or that you, for whatever reason, found useful.

Goatsucker

Old *goatherds swear how all night long they hear
The warning whirr and burring of the bird
Who wakes with darkness and till dawn works hard
Vampiring dry of milk each great goat udder.
5 Moon full, moon dark, the *chary dairy farmer
Dreams that his fattest cattle dwindle, fevered
By claw-cuts of the Goatsucker, alias Devil-bird,
Its eye, flashlit, a chip of ruby fire.

So fables say the Goatsucker moves, masked from men's sight
10 In an ebony air, on wings of witch cloth,
Well-named, ill-famed a knavish fly-by-night,
Yet it never milked any goat, nor dealt cow death
And *shadows only – cave-mouth bristle beset –
*Cockchafers and the *wan, green luna moth.

Sylvia Plath

Glossary

*__goatherd__ – a person who looks after goats (like a shepherd)

*__chary__ – cautiously reluctant

*__shadows__ – to follow

*__cockchafer__ – a type of (flying) beetle

*__wan__ – pale

Read the poem 'Goatsucker' by Sylvia Plath and answer the questions that follow at the appropriate level, using complete sentences.

The marks given for each question a guide as to how much you should write in your answers.

LEVEL 2 questions

1   (a)   What do the goatherds accuse the Goatsucker of doing?   (2)

     (b)   What does it actually do?   (2)

2   How does the poet make the Goatsucker seem hellish?   (8)

3   How do humans react to the Goatsucker? In your answer you should
     write down and explain two quotations.   (4)

4   How does the poet – apart from the description of the Goatsucker –
     create an atmosphere of darkness in the poem?   (4)

5   What do you think the Goatsucker really is? Refer to the text where
     necessary to support your answers.   (5)

LEVEL 1 questions

1   (a)   What do the farmers accuse the Goatsucker of doing?   (2)

    (b)   What does it actually do?   (2)

2   (a)   Write down three quotations that make the Goatsucker sound
          like a devilish creature.   (3)

    (b)   Explain your choices in detail.   (6)

3   The poem mentions goatherds and dairy farmers. Describe what each is
    doing.   (4)

4   Throughout the poem, Plath keeps up an atmosphere of darkness.
    Write down three words or phrases that contribute to this atmosphere,
    but that do not relate directly to the Goatsucker.   (3)

5   What do you think the Goatsucker really is? Refer to the text where
    necessary to support your answers.   (5)

BOTH LEVELS

Write on any ONE of the following topics. Each one is worth 25 marks.

Credit will be given for good spelling, punctuation and presentation, as well as for imaginative and exciting use of language and sentence structure.

1   Write a story that starts with the following sentence: 'Dawn was still hours away and it would be a long night.'

2   Full Tilt

3   Beyond the Horizon

4   Write a story or descriptive piece using one of the following titles:
    - Sand Running Through my Fingers
    - Never Give Up
    - The Team

Practice paper 4

Paper 1, Section A: Literary prose comprehension

Too Soft

The narrator, Amir, is a boy growing up in Afghanistan.

That was how I escaped my father's *aloofness, in my dead mother's books. When I had finished my mother's books, I started spending my allowance on books. I bought one a week from the bookstore near Cinema Park, and stored them in cardboard boxes when I ran out of shelf room.

Of course, marrying a poet was one thing, but fathering a son who preferred burying his face in
5 poetry books to hunting ... well, that wasn't how Baba had envisioned it, I suppose. Real men didn't read poetry – and God forbid they should ever write it! Real men – real boys – played soccer just as Baba had when he had been young. Now *that* was something to be passionate about. He signed me up for soccer teams to stir the same passion in me. But I was pathetic, a blundering liability to my own team, always in the way of an opportune pass or unwittingly blocking an open lane. I shambled
10 about the field on scraggy legs, squalled for passes that never came my way. And the harder I tried, waving my arms over my head frantically and screeching, 'I'm open! I'm open!' the more I went ignored. But Baba wouldn't give up. When it became abundantly clear that I hadn't inherited a shred of his athletic talents, he settled for trying to turn me into a passionate spectator. Certainly I could manage that, couldn't I? I faked interest for as long as possible. I cheered with him when Kabul's
15 team scored against Kandahar and yelped insults at the referee when he called a penalty against our team. But Baba sensed my lack of genuine interest and resigned himself to the bleak fact that his son was never going to either play or watch soccer.

I remember one time Baba took me to the yearly *Buzkashi* tournament that took place on the first day of spring, New Year's Day. *Buzkashi* was, and still is, Afghanistan's national passion.
20 A *chapandaz*, a highly skilled horseman, has to snatch a goat or cattle carcass from the midst of a melee, carry that carcass with him around the stadium at full gallop, and drop it in a scoring circle while a team of other *chapandaz* chases him and does everything in its power – kick, claw, whip, punch – to snatch the carcass from him. That day, the crowd roared with excitement as the horsemen on the field bellowed their battle cries and jostled for the carcass in a cloud of dust. The
25 earth trembled with the clatter of hooves. We watched from the upper bleachers as riders pounded past us at full gallop, yipping and yelling, foam flying from their horses' mouths.

At one point I watched with horror as one of the *chapandaz* fell off his saddle and was trampled under a score of hooves. His body was tossed and hurled in the stampede like a rag doll, finally rolling to a stop when the melee moved on. He twitched once and lay motionless, his legs bent
30 at unnatural angles, a pool of his blood soaking through the sand.

I began to cry.

I cried all the way back home. I remember how Baba's hands clenched around the steering wheel. Clenched and unclenched. Mostly, I will never forget Baba's valiant efforts to conceal the disgusted look on his face as he drove in silence.

(abridged)

Glossary

*aloofness – being cool and distant

Read the passage entitled 'Too Soft' which is taken from The Kite Runner by Khaled Hosseini and answer the questions that follow at the appropriate level, using complete sentences.

The marks given for each question are a guide as to how much you should write in your answer.

LEVEL 2 questions

1   (a)   What is Baba's view of what real men should do?   (3)

     (b)   In what way does Amir disappoint these expectations?   (1)

2   The narrator describes vividly how he tries to play soccer and then how
     he tries to support soccer. Choose one of these episodes and explain
     how the author makes it effective.   (4)

3   How does the author bring the Buzkashi tournament to life?   (6)

4   What is the relationship between Baba and Amir like? In your response,
     you should explain the relationship both from Baba's and Amir's point
     of view.   (6)

5   Do you sympathise more with the father or the narrator in this extract?
     Support your arguments with reference to the text where appropriate.   (5)

1   Look at lines 4–7.

    (a)   What is Baba's, the father's, view of what real men should and should not do?   (3)

    (b)   In what way does his son, the narrator, disappoint these expectations?   (1)

2   Look at lines 7–12, in which the narrator describes how he tries to play soccer.

    (a)   Write down two quotations that show that the son is no good at soccer.   (2)

    (b)   Explain your choices briefly.   (2)

3   Look at lines 18–26 that describe the Buzkashi tournament.

    (a)   Write down two quotations that make the tournament come to life.   (2)

    (b)   Explain your choices in detail.   (4)

4   (a)   Find a quotation that tells you how Amir feels about his father and explain your choice in detail.   (1+2)

    (b)   Find a quotation that tells you how Baba feels about his son and explain your choice in detail.   (1+2)

5   Do you sympathise more with the father or the narrator in this extract? Support your arguments with reference to the text where appropriate.   (5)

Paper 1, Section B: Writing task

BOTH LEVELS

Write on any ONE of the following topics. Each one is worth 25 marks.

Credit will be given for good spelling, punctuation and presentation, as well as for effective use of language and sentence structure.

1   What is your favourite possession? Write a letter to a friend in which you try to persuade him or her to also acquire your possession.

2   How do you prepare for a long journey or a long time away? Explain in detail what steps you take and why they are useful.

3   We live in the best of times. Discuss this statement, using examples wherever necessary.

4   EITHER

    (a)   Do you like reading books in which one of the leading characters is an animal? Explain your point of view, using one or more books you have read to help argue your point.

    OR

    (b)   Do you like an outwardly strong main character or do you prefer one who seems more troubled and weak? Explain your point of view, using books you have read to support your ideas.

The True History of Resurrection Jack

Resurrection Jack lay under a stone
curled like a grub and quite alone
he was three weeks old and his skin was black
and he didn't even know his name was Jack

5 Bare was the *veldt and hard as bone
where he lay beneath his burying-stone
ditched by a mother who grudged him breath
but that little baby gave the slip to death

White folk passing heard a sound
10 thought it was coming out of the ground
paused to listen and heard a moan
tracked poor Jack and rolled that stone

Raised him up in the eye of the sun
and that was the day when his life begun
15 he went with the white folk and never looked back
and they grew together though his skin was black

He lived long years till his life was done
with the folk who'd lifted him into the sun
for there's things go deeper than white or black

20 and that's the true tale of Resurrection Jack

Evangeline Paterson

Glossary

*veldt – wide open country side

Read the poem 'The True History of Resurrection Jack' by Evangeline Paterson and answer the questions that follow at the appropriate level, using complete sentences.

The marks given for each question are a guide as to how much you should write in your answer.

LEVEL 2 questions

1   Briefly retell the story of Resurrection Jack's life in your own words, as told by the poem.   (4)

2   The poem lacks all punctuation and most capital letters. Why do you think the author writes this way?   (3)

3   How does the poet bring her story to life?   (6)

4   Comment on the rhythm and rhyme, as well as stanza structure, of the poem.   (6)

5   With close reference to the text, explain why you think Jack was called 'Resurrection Jack'. In your answer, use quotations from the text to explain your ideas.   (6)

LEVEL 1 questions

1   Retell the story of Resurrection Jack's life.   (6)

2   Do you think the fact that the poem has no punctuation and very few
     capital letters makes it easier or harder to read? Explain your opinion.   (2)

3   (a)   Write down three quotations that bring the story of Resurrection
            Jack to life.   (3)

     (b)   Explain your choices in detail.   (6)

4   (a)   The poem has a regular rhyme scheme of always two lines
            rhyming (rhyming couplets). What does this add to the poem?   (2)

     (b)   The poem has a strong rhythm. How does this make the poem
            more effective?   (2)

5   Write down two quotations from the poem to show why you think Jack
     was called Resurrection Jack. Explain them briefly.   (2+2)

BOTH LEVELS

Write on any ONE of the following topics. Each one is worth 25 marks.

Credit will be given for good spelling, punctuation and presentation, as well as for imaginative and exciting use of language.

1   Write a description of a place you only ever saw from far away, but wished you could have seen from closer.

2   The Canvas of the Mind

3   Write a story or descriptive piece using one of the following titles:
   • Starry Night
   • Two Steps Forward, One Step Back
   • Midnight Feast

4   Forget Grammar!

Practice paper 5

The Salem Witch Trials Begin

A number of girls in Salem are pretending that other inhabitants are casting spells on them. Ringleader of the girls is Abigail, with whom Proctor had a brief affair. A court has been set up to investigate the claims of witchcraft. Proctor's wife Elizabeth is telling him that their maid, Mary Warren, is at the court in Salem.

ELIZABETH: Mary Warren's there today.

PROCTOR: Why'd you let her? You heard me forbid her go to Salem any more.

ELIZABETH: I couldn't stop her.

PROCTOR [*holding back a full condemnation of her*]: *It* is a fault, it is a fault, Elizabeth – you're the
5 mistress here, not Mary Warren.

ELIZABETH: She frightened all my strength away.

PROCTOR: How may that mouse frighten you, Elizabeth? You–

ELIZABETH: It is a mouse no more. I forbid her go, and she raises up her chin like the daughter of a prince and says to me, 'I must go to Salem, Goody Proctor; I am an official of the court!'

10 PROCTOR: Court! What court?

ELIZABETH: Aye, it is a proper court they have now. They've sent four judges out of Boston, she says, weighty magistrates of the General Court, and at the head sits the Deputy Governor of the Province.

PROCTOR [*astonished*]: Why, she's mad.

ELIZABETH: I would to God she were. There be fourteen people in the jail now, she says.

15 [*PROCTOR simply looks at her, unable to grasp it.*]

And they'll be tried, and the court have power to hang them too, she says.

PROCTOR [*scoffing, but without conviction*]: Ah, they'd never hang–

ELIZABETH: The Deputy Governor promise hangin' if they'll not confess, John. The town's gone wild, I think. She speak of Abigail, and I thought she were a saint, to hear her. Abigail brings the other girls
20 into the court, and where she walks the crowd will part like the sea for Israel. And folks are brought before them, and if they scream and howl and fall to the floor – the person's clapped in the jail for bewitchin' them.

PROCTOR [*wide-eyed*]: Oh, it is a black mischief.

ELIZABETH: I think you must go to Salem, John.

25 [*He turns to her.*]

I think so. You must tell them it is a fraud.

PROCTOR [*thinking beyond this*]: Aye, it is, it is surely.

ELIZABETH: Let you go to Ezekiel Cheever – he knows you well. And tell him what she said to you last week in her uncle's house. She said it had naught to do with witchcraft, did she not?

30 PROCTOR [*in thought*]: Aye, she did, she did.

[*Now, a pause.*]

ELIZABETH [*quietly jeering to anger him by prodding*]: God forbid you keep that from the court, John. I think they must be told.

PROCTOR *[quietly, struggling with his thought]:* Aye, they must, they must. It is a wonder they
35 do believe her.

ELIZABETH: I would go to Salem now, John – let you go tonight.

PROCTOR: I'll think on it.

ELIZABETH *[with her courage now]:* You cannot keep it, John.

PROCTOR *[angering]:* I know I cannot keep it. I say I will think on it!

40 ELIZABETH *[hurt, and very coldly]:* Good, then, let you think on it. *[She stands and starts to walk out of the room.]*

PROCTOR: I am only wondering how I may prove what she told me, Elizabeth. If the girl's a saint now, I think it is not easy to prove she's fraud, and the town gone so silly. She told it to me in a room alone – I have no proof for it.

45 ELIZABETH *[with a smile, to keep her dignity]:* John, if it were not Abigail that you must go to hurt, would you falter now? I think not.

PROCTOR: Now look you –

ELIZABETH: I see what I see, John.

PROCTOR *[with solemn warning]:* You will not judge me more, Elizabeth. I have good reason to think
50 before I charge fraud on Abigail, and I will think on it. Let you look to your own improvement before you go to judge your husband any more.

    (abridged)

Read the passage entitled 'The Salem Witch Trials Begin' which is taken from Act Two of The Crucible *by Arthur Miller and answer the questions that follow at the appropriate level, using complete sentences.*

The marks given for each question are a guide as to how much you should write in your answer.

LEVEL 2 questions

1   What news from Salem does Elizabeth tell Proctor?   (4)

2   (a)   What does Elizabeth say about Abigail's appearance at court?   (3)

      (b)   What does this tell you about Abigail?   (2)

3   Why is Proctor reluctant to go to Salem?   (6)

4   Proctor and Elizabeth are husband and wife; what do you learn about their relationship with one another?   (6)

5   Look at the stage directions. What is their role? Choose two and explain their function and necessity.   (4)

LEVEL 1 questions

1 What is the news from Salem that Elizabeth tells Proctor? (4)

2 Look at lines 20–22.

   (a) What does Elizabeth say about how Abigail behaved in court? (3)

   (b) What does this tell you about Abigail? (2)

3 (a) Find two quotations from lines 27–51 that show that Proctor does not want to go to Salem. (2)

   (b) Explain what each quotation tells you about the reasons Proctor does not want to go. (4)

4 (a) Write down two quotations that tell you that the relationship between Proctor and Elizabeth is not a happy one. (2)

   (b) Explain your choices in detail. (4)

5 (a) Look at the stage direction in line 25. What is its purpose? (2)

   (b) Look at the stage direction in line 39. What is its purpose? (2)

Paper 1, Section B: Writing task

BOTH LEVELS

Write on any ONE of the following topics. Each one is worth 25 marks.

Credit will be given for good spelling, punctuation and presentation, as well as for appropriate use of style and language.

1   Write a speech to be delivered in front of the whole school about what each pupil can do to help save the environment.

2   'Sticks and stones may break my bones, but names will never hurt me.' Have you ever been in a situation where you had to remind yourself or someone else of this saying? Write about your experience, making it as detailed and clear as possible.

3   Life is too short to spend it doing things you don't want to. Discuss this statement, highlighting both sides of the issue and using examples where appropriate.

4   EITHER

   (a)   A lot of books, like detective novels, have a mystery or riddle that needs to be solved and that you can attempt to solve as you read. Explain with reference to one or more books you have read, whether or not you like this kind of book.

       OR

   (b)   'Some books are undeservedly forgotten; none are undeservedly remembered.' (W. H. Auden)
Have you read a book that you think should be forgotten, or one that deserves to be remembered?

Especially When It Snows

(for Boty)

especially when it snows
and every tree
has its dark arms and widespread hands
full of that shining angelfood

5 especially when it snows
and every footprint
makes a dark lake
among the frozen grass

especially when it snows darling
10 and tough little robins
beg for crumbs
at golden-spangled windows

ever since we said goodbye to you
in that memorial garden
15 where nothing grew
except the beautiful blank-eyed snow

and little Caitlin crouched to wave goodbye to you
down in the shadows

especially when it snows
20 and keeps on snowing

especially when it snows
and down the purple pathways of the sky
the planet staggers like King Lear
with his dead darling in his arms

25 especially when it snows
and keeps on snowing

　　　Adrian Mitchell

Read the poem 'Especially When It Snows' by Adrian Mitchell and answer the questions that follow at the appropriate level, using complete sentences.

The marks given for each question are a guide as to how much you should write in your answers.

LEVEL 2 questions

1   (a)   Who is the poet speaking to in the poem?   (2)

       (b)   Who do you think this could be?   (2)

2   How does the writer make the description of winter effective?   (6)

3   Comment on the poet's use of repetition in the poem. In what way is it effective?   (4)

4   How does the poet create a mood of grief and loss in the second part of the poem (lines 13–24)?   (6)

5   In the poem we are never told what happens especially when it snows. What do you think it is? Use quotations from the text to support your ideas.   (5)

1 (a) The poem is addressed to Boty. Who do you think this could be? (2)

   (b) Who do you think Caitlin is (line 17)? (2)

2 (a) Write down three quotations from lines 1–12 that you think are particularly effective in making the description of winter vivid. (3)

   (b) Explain your choices in detail. (6)

3 The poet repeats the phrase 'especially when it snows' throughout the poem. In what way is this effective? (2)

4 In lines 13–24 the poet creates a mood of grief and loss.

   (a) Write down two quotations that bring out this mood. (2)

   (b) Explain your choices in detail. (4)

5 The poet does not tell us what happens when it snows. What do you happens? Give reasons for your answer. (4)

Paper 2, Section B: Writing task

BOTH LEVELS

Write on any ONE of the following topics. Each one is worth 25 marks.

Credit will be given for good spelling, punctuation and presentation, as well as for imaginative and exciting use of language and sentence structure.

1   Write in any way you like on one of the following:
    - Believe in Magic
    - The Experiment
    - Copycat

2   Describe a location where you stopped by accident. Apart from explaining the circumstances that brought you there, try to bring the place and your experience of being there to life.

3   The Hunt

4   Write a story that includes someone saying the following words: 'I think we got away there.'